IMPROVE YOUR
SKIING

IMPROVE YOUR SKIING

Willow Books
Collins
8 Grafton Street, London W1
1987

Willow Books
William Collins Sons & Co Ltd
London · Glasgow · Sydney · Auckland
Toronto · Johannesburg

First published 1987
© Sackville Design Group Ltd

BRITISH LIBRARY CATALOGUING IN PUBLICATION DATA
Improve your Skiing
1. Skis and skiing
796.93   GV854

ISBN 0-00-218258-0

Designed by Sackville Design Group Ltd
78 Margaret Street, London W1N 7HB
Editorial consultant: Konrad Bartelski
Art director: Phil Evans
In-house editor: Lorraine Jerram
Illustrations: Phil Evans
Jill Evans
Chris Martin
Set in Melior by Optima Typographic, Wembley
Printed and bound in Italy by New Interlitho S.P.A. Milan

Contents

Successful skiing

I was fortunate to have been introduced to the pleasure of sliding down the beautiful white mountains almost at the same time as I had mastered the art of walking. Initially, the cold, snowy winter world seemed a trifle hostile from where I could see it, although it was not long before the excitement of having a new-found freedom to race around the slopes overcame my initial caution. I slotted straight into the expert guidance of the Kitzbühel ski school, and quickly found an environment that was easily more stimulating than the routine of the classroom.

Having spent my early days in the expert hands of the ski instructors, the 'Red Devils' of Kitz, it was then one of my greatest thrills to return, six years later, as a competitor on the gruelling Hannenkahm World Cup downhill, even if I did end up in the fences a few times! It gives me a thrill, too, that so many people are recognizing what a great holiday and sport skiing can be at all levels. Whether skiing downhill or cross-country, everyone can enjoy the impressive scenery of the glistening white mountain peaks. It is one of the few sports that the whole family can experience together.

This book dispels the myth that skiing is difficult. Learning to ski is easy when you take it stage by stage. If you follow the clear, easy steps detailed here, you will be positively enjoying yourself on the slopes and this, of course, is the easiest way to improve. This book is written to help you *feel* what is happening on the slopes. You do not need to memorize or follow every one of the points, but remembering some will help things slot into place more quickly.

Many novice skiers are bemused by the different teaching methods offered by the national ski schools. All these have their advantages, but this book stems from practising skiers and their own personal experiences. The book's contributors share in common a love of the sport, the snow and the magic of the mountains. But even these experts know that no matter how much training and preparation you put in, you can still find yourself landing on your head. Just as each snowflake is unique, so is each day's skiing. It is always a different experience from which you may learn something new. Some of the great names – Mueller, Stenmark, Walliser, for example – will freely admit that they are always learning. So whether you are at the top of your class or on the nursery slopes for the first time ever, learning is part of doing; it is part of the fun.

Remember, too, that with skiing you can progress at your own pace, extending yourself little by little – because you are competing with no one but yourself. A lot of people are self-conscious about other skiers and what they might think of mistakes. You may rest assured that they are too busy with their own enjoyment to be much concerned about anybody else!

As anyone who has taken up this sport will confirm, skiing is not simply sliding down mountains; it is a way of life. It may revolve around the slopes but an integral part of the sport's attraction is the social atmosphere in which it takes place. Not only are there scenic marvels to be visited but there are organized parties or social events almost every evening. Your off-the-slopes activities can be as lively or as relaxed as you wish – but then you probably do not need me to tell you about après-ski . . .

KONRAD BARTELSKI

Konrad Bartelski achieved the highest ever placing of a British skier in a World Cup downhill – he came second in the race at Val Gardena in 1981. Since retiring in 1983, his love of skiing has kept him active in many different areas of the sport

To be on top of a mountain in brilliant sunshine with crisp snow at your feet is, for most people, the essence of skiing. This is only one of the many sensations and experiences that make the sport so dangerously addictive. To be there well-equipped and well-prepared can only add to the pleasure and to your chances of skiing well. This means not simply equipping yourself with hardware that slides and turns easily, but also dressing intelligently for protection against changing weather conditions. Confidence is what it is all about and, fortunately, this has become much less of a hurdle than it once was. Today's skiers are lucky enough to be able to take advantage of a century's thought, invention and development of ski technology.

Choosing your boots

Ski boots are argued over, worried about and fussed around more than any other aspect of ski equipment. This is hardly surprising. City and suburban feet are not accustomed to being locked into a plastic shell for eight hours a day and often have something to say about it shortly after a ski holiday starts. That said, comfort is less elusive than it once was. Plastic boots are nearly always dry inside; leather boots rarely used to be. Modern rear-entry boots are much easier to put on and somewhat easier to walk in, though there is still progress to be made in this area.

When choosing ski boots it is as well to understand their function because many boots provide unsatisfactory performance. Boots are the link between your skiing movements, almost all of which should be in the knees and ankles, and your skis. Stand up for a moment with this book and, with your feet two or three feet apart, press lightly on one foot. Tip your leg from side to side, forwards and backwards. The ankle joint will allow a considerable amount of rocking and tipping action, with your foot staying almost flat on the floor. The ankle joint was not designed for skiing.

A ski boot stiffens much of the ankle's movement, providing the lower leg with a little forward lean – good for a balanced position over the skis – and locking most of the ankle's side-to-side movement. The 'spoiler' at the back of the boot helps prevent you from falling backwards. The skiing movements of your leg are transmitted by the boot to the sole of the ski, making the ski steer or slide. Think of your lower leg and the shaft of the boot as a joystick and your understanding of skiing will already have the edge over most people's. It is essentially the driving of the leg and boot forwards, and to the left and right, that changes a ski's direction most efficiently.

Buying boots
After one or two ski trips it is as well to buy your own boots. With a little care at the time of purchase you will be more comfortable and you will be sure of what you are using from year to year.

Aim for a standard of boot beyond your present abilities. The differences between an expert's require-

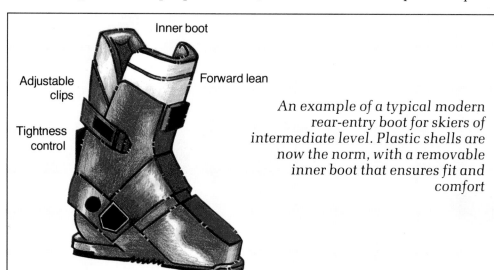

Inner boot

Forward lean

Adjustable clips

Tightness control

An example of a typical modern rear-entry boot for skiers of intermediate level. Plastic shells are now the norm, with a removable inner boot that ensures fit and comfort

Competitive skiers depend heavily on the performance and reliability of their equipment. Downhill racers such as Peter Mueller of Switzerland wear boots that allow for exact force transmission from foot to ski

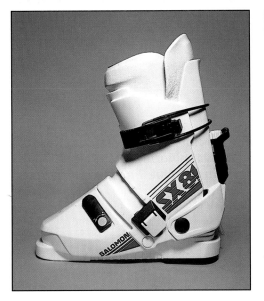

Ski boots need careful selection. There is a wide range currently available and new boots should always be tried out. Today's models have a variety of adjustable attachments (above and far left) and some even have a custom-foamed inner boot (left) to provide optimum comfort

Choosing your boots

ments and those of an intermediate are less obvious than they used to be. Most experts use softer flexing boots than they used to and most intermediates are better off with stiffer boots than they might normally choose. At one time the expert's boot was higher than the intermediate's for extra support. This distinction is not important nowadays.

Ski shops vary considerably in their ability to fit boots and you should find a shop that is prepared to spend some time looking after your individual needs. Set aside at least half a day for buying boots and visit shops when they are well-stocked (early in the season) and quiet (not Saturdays). Find out who the best-qualified fitter in the shop is and ask for his or her help.

There are two basic forms of boot – front-entry and rear-entry. Front-entry boots are still popular with some experts and racers for their close fit. They have a traditional design with overlapping sides to the shell and a row of clips to pull the shell tight. Like an ordinary shoe or boot, a tongue is pulled out in order to enter the boot.

Rear-entry boots have swept the market in recent years because they are easier to use. The back section of the shell opens so that the foot can slide in quickly. It can be left part-open for extra ankle movement when standing or walking to the lifts. Whereas front-entry boots vary little in design, rear-entry boots have undergone considerable innovation. It is a good idea to compare different designs for their different features – you will want to try a number of boots for comfort and fit anyway.

Check the fit and comfort

With modern fitting techniques, which enable a good fitter to adapt a boot to your foot, almost anyone should be able to get a comfortable boot.

Off-the-shelf comfort should be accepted cautiously. It is easy for a boot manufacturer to pad the interior with soft foam which will feel soft and cosy but which will also absorb movement. The cuffs of many boots are also very soft and pliable to provide extra comfort but, again, a compromise in performance is created.

Unless you are a beginner, when you will want the maximum comfort during all the awkward movements you will be asked to make, avoid the padded boots. A better bet is to find a model with firmer padding and a reasonably stiff cuff and, if necessary, have the boot modified to your foot.

Although rear-entry boots have become popular in recent years (far left), front-entry models (left) are still favoured by some experts and racers for their valuable close fit

When trying on boots, check the fit with the following points:

1 Get your feet measured in the shop – use your normal shoe size as a guide only. The fitter should also be measuring or examining the height of your instep, width of foot and any other characteristics that will lead you to the right model or size.

2 Put on stretch ski socks with a high wool content, but not the thick ribbed variety. They should be high enough to reach above the boot cuff.

3 Wear different boots on each foot for comparison. Flex and tilt the boots, walk around and hop in them. If you feel any numbness or pressure points tell the fitter.

An example of a 'moving mountain'

4 Your toes can touch the front of the boot very lightly when you are standing straight but with a little forward pressure they should move back and should be free to wiggle.

The most important controls and clips on a boot close the shell and tighten the foot within it. Other adjustments include the angle of forward lean – not very important – and the softness or hardness of the forward flex – very useful. The simplest and most effective form of flex control is a sliding wedge over the instep which blocks, to varying degrees, the amount the boot shaft can tilt for-wards. It means you can tune the boot's flexibility to your weight, strength and tastes. If the boot is a rear-entry, try opening the top clip. This should allow easy walking.

Standard boots do not fit everyone comfortably and manufacturers of boots and fitting accessories have come up with many useful remedies.

The most thorough tailor-made fit is the custom-foamed inner boot. While you stand in the boot two chemicals are shaken in a bottle and the reaction creates a rubbery foam. The foam forces itself through plastic tubes that enter the boot shell and feed into a bladder in the inner boot. Similarly, many people with arch problems are helped by 'orthotic' in-soles. These are usually heated and softened and placed under the feet to mould them into the right shape.

The inner liner on some boots can be thinned at pressure points with a small electric grinder. Alternatively, the boot shell can be heated and stretched. The fit of a ski boot can be tightened in specific areas by sticking self-adhesive foam pads at the appro-priate points.

Testing new boots
The more you can do to try new boots before you 'break them in' on the mountain the better. Some ski shops have installed a machine called a 'moving mountain' which is an excellent way to try out new boots. The skier makes short movements on mini skis on a revolving carpet.

Alternatively, take the boots to an artificial ski slope. An hour's practice should indicate whether you are like-ly to run into problems with them.

Choosing your skis

A recent ski adventure film included an exciting sequence in which the main character skied a mogul field on nothing but his boots. Apart from demonstrating that skis can be fun in any length, or even no length, it shows that skis could be thought of as a turning agent of the boot. A ski boot could, as mentioned before, also be described as a joystick in the way it controls a ski. Applying pressure from the shin to the front of the boot and tilting it sets the ski on edge. It is then that the dynamic qualities of the ski take over. The ski performs a carved turn in this situation, an efficient way of maintaining speed while changing direction.

Skis are designed to carve turns with very little force. The ski has a narrow section at the centre – the waist – and the edges are curved from the tip and tail towards the waist. Once pressure is applied to the centre of the ski's edge it bends and the ski simply rides its curved side. Like a train on a curved section of track the ski has to turn. Now, imagine the inconceivable – a train that skids. In real life this is how every skier uses his skis. Racers skid very little – if they did not carve through the course they would turn too late, skid, and miss a gate.

Many recreational skiers spend a ski career having never carved a turn. It is a pity because skidding is actually harder work but it is the 'natural' way to ski if lessons have been abandoned at an early stage. (See also Chapter 3.)

What does all this have to do with ski design? Essentially a ski that will be skidded has to be made in a different way to one that will be carved. In other words, it has to be 'forgiving' and is made to twist and flatten out at the tail when the centre is put on edge. So in any manufacturer's range there are skis that carve more (racing skis) and skis that skid more (forgiving recreational skis). Judge your own skiing objectively and decide which ones you deserve!

Ski construction is becoming more complex and precise as the quest for the 'perfect' ski continues. Depending on its performance level and price, a ski contains a number of layers to control its performance. Most skis contain either a foam plastic core or a laminated wood core. The main aim of the core is to separate the layers of glass or carbon fibre that actually give a ski its strength and resilience. To control vibrations, which can reduce a ski's contact and hold on ice, there are often thin layers of rubber or visco-elastic material.

The ski's base and steel edges are the most tangible evidence of its role. The base, made from polyethylene, makes the ski slide by pressure-melting the snow surface. It must be maintained in perfect condition – as must the edges – in order to ensure good performance.

Buying skis

First you need to know the type of ski

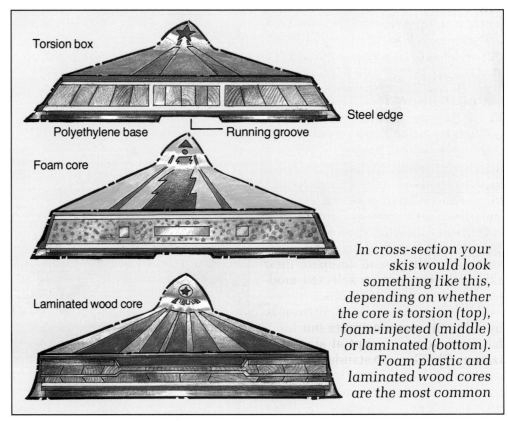

Torsion box

Polyethylene base — Running groove

Steel edge

Foam core

Laminated wood core

In cross-section your skis would look something like this, depending on whether the core is torsion (top), foam-injected (middle) or laminated (bottom). Foam plastic and laminated wood cores are the most common

Marc Girardelli of Luxembourg
weaves his way down a demanding
super-G course by carving turns
through the gates. Racing skis are
designed to minimize skidding

that is best suited to your abilities and then buy it in the length that suits your weight, height and the speed at which you like to ski.

There is a lot of mystique when it comes to shopping for skis and many shops like to substitute it for real advice. Ski salesmen are on the end of a chain of marketing enthusiasm dispensed by the manufacturers and are all too willing to dispense opinions. Ask a ski salesman to put his hand on his heart and say how many of the skis he has actually used and you may get a blank stare. If he can show you independent test results then he is worth knowing.

How much should you spend? A new pair of skis will not transform your technique. A similar outlay on private lessons with a top instructor could. Unless you are a connoisseur of the finer points of performance, buy skis that fall within the mid-price bracket. Spend £50 more and you are likely to gain only a marginal improvement in performance.

If they are your first skis choose a budget pair and make sure the bindings are good enough to be transferred to your second pair of skis. And make sure, too, that the bulk of your outlay at this stage has gone on a top quality pair of boots. For the best deal on skis visit a few shops and compare their ski package prices on selected models, which include bindings.

Ski abilities are defined differently by different manufacturers but there has been some attempt at standardization. The German standards organization DIN has defined ski abilities at three levels and some ski manufacturers (notably Austrian) use the

Choosing your skis

codings on their skis: 'S' stands for experts who can handle all slopes at all speeds; 'A' stands for intermediates who ski moderate gradients at medium speeds; 'L' stands for beginners and learners who ski on easy slopes at slow speeds.

The vast majority of skis are made for recreational skiers who have no particular racing ambitions. There are also a lot of skis with racing cosmetics made to flatter holiday skiers! Most of the top manufacturers make excellent models and there is often little to choose between them in terms of performance. Look for test results on the latest models in ski magazines. If you particularly like skiing powder look for a slightly softer ski, vice versa if you only ski on piste.

Because a ski supports your weight it is important not to over-flex it or under-flex it. Your weight should be spread evenly along the ski and not concentrated at the tip, tail or centre as it will be if you are not correctly loading it.

Most ski manufacturers give height recommendations for each model and these should be followed. However, if you are thin or overweight subtract up to ten centimetres or add up to ten centimetres respectively. As a general rule start skiing on skis between head height and ten centimetres below it. Then take ten-centimetre steps upwards as your ability and speed improve. The maximum length most recreational expert skiers use is thirty centimetres above head height.

Your choice of ski may be determined by the type of terrain on which you intend to ski

The camber (top), top surface (middle) and bottom surface of a ski .

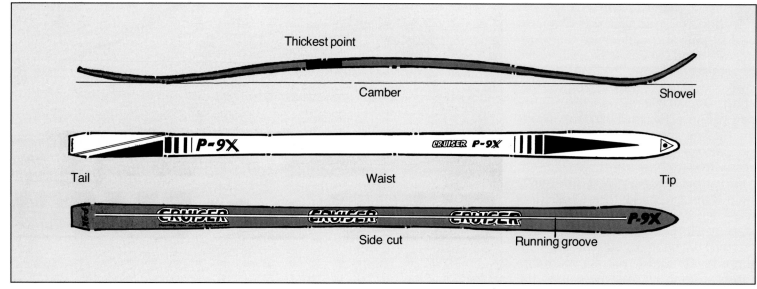

Thickest point

Camber

Shovel

P-9X CRUISER P-9X

Tail

Waist

Tip

Side cut

Running groove

Maintaining your skis

It is tragic to see the damage done to skis when conditions are bad. The soles and edges of a ski are very vulnerable to rock damage and the ski's performance will deteriorate every time it scrapes over a rocky surface.

Admittedly, ski soles have become much harder in recent times – the result of the widespread use of compressed 'sintered' plastic to make them. But ski edges are very easily blunted. The only answer is to rent skis when the pistes are bare, particularly if your skis are new or nearly new. The rental shop will already have costed the expected damage into their charges – you cannot do the same with your own skis and it could be an expensive and futile exercise to use them, especially since you will not be able to enjoy them fully anyway. Save them for a snowy day!

Having said that, damage is inevitable however careful you are. Repairing damage and tuning skis is a specialized art but it is not beyond the ability of a competent do-it-yourself enthusiast.

Filing skis and edges
A ski's base must be perfectly flat from edge to edge to give it the best sliding and turning performance. A 25cm/10in single cut file will 'flat file' the base; press it flat on the base and push it down the ski. Shops generally do this job with a revolving belt sander or stone grinder.

A useful tool to buy is an edge tuning tool which sets the correct angle between the bottom and side of the edge. This is quite easy to use and can produce sharp edges for icy conditions – a valuable asset.

Repairing bases
This used to be a fairly straightforward exercise involving dripping molten 'Ptex' from a burning candle and scraping the base smooth. This method can still be used on the new hard bases but it is not ideal – the repair plastic will be much softer than the rest of the base.

Waxing
The best waxing method is to use an electric or gas iron and to smooth the molten wax along the base before scraping it down to a fine, smooth film. More economical on wax is to place a sheet of tissue paper under the iron and smooth the wax over the base. This method should not require scraping.

Waxing your skis not only makes them run faster, but also makes them easier to turn

Ski bindings

As its name suggests, a ski binding holds the ski boot firmly to the ski. For the greater part of this century, ski bindings did little more than that: in a fall the binding simply helped the ski perform a rather unpleasant mangling exercise on the leg. It is hardly surprising, therefore, that skiing still has to shake off its 'broken leg' image.

The past thirty years, however, have seen the rise and refinement of the 'release binding', a device that virtually guarantees that the ski will not apply dangerous pressure on the leg. Provided that the binding has been correctly set to the size of boot, and adjusted to the correct tension setting, it can almost be taken for granted.

Today there are remarkably few manufacturers of ski bindings – only five prominent ones, compared to over fifty ski manufacturers. Many newcomers have tried to enter the market but have failed; their fancy engineering concepts simply confused the issue. The crucial ingredient of a good ski binding is a simple failsafe mechanism that will survive icing up, wear and tear, and impact.

The majority of bindings work with a unit that holds the boot's toe and a separate unit that holds the heel. In a twisting fall the toe unit opens sideways; in a forward fall the heel unit opens upwards. This might seem straightforward but it disguises a complex calculation of forces, their duration and their direction. A binding is a decision-making mechanism and it has to make the right decision every time: to release or not to release; whether or not the leg is threatened. It

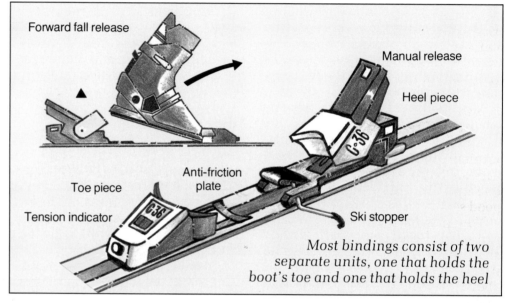

Most bindings consist of two separate units, one that holds the boot's toe and one that holds the heel

may be dangerous not to release from a binding but it is also aggravating (and possibly hazardous) to release from a binding inadvertently.

To make the right decision the binding allows itself a 'grey area' by incorporating a shock-absorbing mechanism. If the ski shudders hard and quickly the binding will begin to open, the boot will shift off-centre but the binding's springs will return it. The shock-absorbing, or retention, qualities of bindings are therefore very important.

Buying bindings

All ski bindings made by the large manufacturers are approved by international test organizations. In terms of safety there is not a great deal to choose between them.

Bindings are calibrated to suit skiers of different weights and speeds. The first step in choosing a binding is to get to know your DIN setting. This is the setting you will see on a numerical scale on any binding. Consult individual binding manufacturers' charts to see how they arrive at your DIN setting. In theory they all agree, but in practice they do not and you may find that you need a DIN setting one or two points up or down between manufacturers – a point to remember if you swap skis with a friend.

Buy bindings beyond your immediate needs. As your skiing progresses and speeds up you may want slightly more advanced bindings. Anticipate this, especially if you are buying a ski package, by buying the next binding model up. The ski shop should be able to sell you the package with a superior binding for a modest supplement. You can then transfer the bindings to your next pair of skis – cheaper than having to buy better bindings the second time around.

Ski poles

Ski poles are a straightforward purchase. The main choice lies in the type of handle, which may or may not include a strap. Straps have gone in and out of fashion but most skiers like them because they provide a firm support for the hand when gripping the handle.

Avoid poles made from cheap aluminium since these bend too easily. Instead, buy a pair made from a good quality alloy – they should give you good service, lasting many years.

Your pole length can be checked by turning a pole upside down. Grip the shaft immediately under the basket (to subtract the short length of pole above the hand, which would normally be in the snow). In this position your forearm should be horizontal.

When buying ski poles, remember to check the length. Your forearm should be parallel to the ground when the inverted pole is gripped under the basket

Whichever type of ski pole you choose, it is important to get the correct length. Poles that are either too long or short will adversely affect your pole planting ability. Ingemar Stenmark of Sweden uses his pole plant to good effect in the slalom

Dressing to ski

Mountains are not places that take kindly to casual dressers. At times, particularly in spring, it can be tempting to leave a ski hat at home or not to wear a ski jacket – you would be ill-advised to do so. Always err on the cautious side. Mountains have a habit of exaggerating bad weather and throwing it at you when you least expect it. A gentle snowfall in a valley can be a howling blizzard 1,000 metres above. Similarly, conditions can change from a blaze of sunshine to a freezing white-out in a matter of minutes.

On the other hand, no one enjoys skiing with a lot of bulky clothing – it is heavy and restricts movement – so the key to effective dressing is to layer it. Start with a vest and tights or long johns. Those made from a stretch weave or polypropylene are of proven value in cold sports. They transmit sweat to the outside of the garment. A T-shirt (or two) above the vest will help absorb any sweat that leaves it, and then a roll-neck shirt made from pure cotton (a classic item of skiwear) will be very effective in keeping the neck warm. Outside this there should be a high-quality woollen ski sweater. These are not cheap, but if you plan to ski a lot they are a worthwhile investment. Buy one with a close knit that has good stretch qualities.

The major investment in skiwear is a suit, or separate jacket and ski pants (or salopettes, the dungaree version). Here the choice is enormous and it is worth remembering a few practical points that ought to override fashion considerations:

1 How tough is the fabric? And how well are the seams stitched? Some of

The golden rule when dressing to ski is to be prepared for anything.
Wear layers so that you can regulate body heat

the most expensive skiwear is made from the weakest fabrics. In a ski shop, ask for the clothing buyer who should be well versed in the relative qualities of different fabrics. In many cases the thickness and density of the fabric will be self-evident. However, if you cannot get any constructive advice, shop elsewhere.

2 How windproof and waterproof is the fabric? The appearance of Gore-Tex has revolutionized the skiwear industry and it is now one of several membranes or coatings that can be laminated on to the base fabric to 'proof' it, while allowing sweat to escape. If the fabric's fibre is woven densely enough, and is water-resist-

ant in nature, this itself will create a weather-beating garment.

3 How many pockets are there? How many do you need? Check that the pockets are large enough to hold the items that you will always be carrying: wallet, sunglasses, sun cream and so on. Some pockets are better placed than others.

4 What type of hood is there? Pull it out and tie it around your head. Does it enclose the head tightly. Does it turn with your head?

5 Are the zips easy to use? The handles should be easy to grab with a gloved hand.

6 How well insulated is it? The latest forms of polyester padding provide good insulation with relatively little bulk. If you plan to ski at various times of the season, with widely varying temperatures, it is better not to buy a thick jacket or suit but to pile on extra layers underneath. However, whatever you choose make sure it has a windproof outer 'shell'.

7 Finally, always check skiwear for its freedom of movement. Swing your arms around, up and down, bend and stretch, and make sure that the jacket or pants move with you. If you really want full isolation from the weather and snow, a one-piece suit (like an overall) is very comfortable.

The last areas where you will need specialist skiwear are the extremities – head, hands and feet. The head carries much of your blood supply close to the surface and loses heat at a rapid rate. It can be very pleasant in milder conditions to ski with the wind rushing through your hair but most of the time you will probably want to wear a hat. It should cover one time ski socks were used as much to pad out and insulate ski boots as they were to provide basic comfort. Nowadays ski boots are well insulated and padded and the sock is used to provide even cushioning against the skin, while absorbing sweat. The little extra warmth is an added bonus. Choose socks with a high wool content that reach a few inches above the height of the boot, and make sure they have good stretch qualities.

Skiwear can be functional and stylish

the ears completely and, for extra warmth, should be woollen rather than acrylic.

Even the most hardy skiers do not ski without gloves. If you are very sensitive to the cold, or are just starting skiing, mittens are also a good bet. Whatever you buy make sure it is well made. Although water-resistant fabrics are now widely used in glove manufacture, leather is still by far the toughest material. A top quality pair of leather gloves, with full reinforcement between thumb and forefinger, and tough stitching, can last a decade. A medium-priced pair of fabric-panelled gloves could be falling to pieces in a fortnight. £40 might seem extortionate for a pair of gloves but it could be the best ski investment you will ever make.

Finally, the question of socks. At

The skier's checklist

Packing for a ski holiday means remembering a multitude of small, but essential, items. It is a lot easier if you have a checklist. Use this one as a basis for your own personal list:

Ski clothes
Ski pants and jacket (or suit)
Ski socks
Thermal underwear
Vests
T-shirts
Handkerchiefs
Roll-neck shirts
Ski sweater
Ski gloves
Ski hat
Après-ski boots

Equipment
Skis
Ski boots
Ski poles
Ski wax
Binding adjustment tool
Goggles
Sunglasses

Essential papers
Passport
Tickets
Foreign currency
Travellers' cheques/ Eurocheques
Credit cards

Clothes
Most people take a small selection of casual clothes. Hotels and chalets are usually well heated. Include:
Jeans/trousers
Shirts
Sweater
Nightclothes
Swimming trunks
Any other clothes (your choice!)

Miscellaneous
Lightweight backpack/bumbag
Washing powder
Radio/cassette player
Photo for lift pass
Alarm clock
Camera
Toiletries
Sun cream
Lip salve
Safety pins
Nail scissors
Sewing kit
Pens and writing paper

Ski lifts

The fastest and most exciting way up a mountain is to jump on an aircraft – a light plane or helicopter will do nicely! These are certainly modes of transport to be sampled at least once in a ski career if you can, just for the thrill of reaching remote powder-covered slopes and exciting descents. However, unless you are rich enough to take this kind of transport for granted you will spend your skiing days being hauled up mountains by loops of cable strung with various components: chairs, cabins, poles with buttons (called a 'Poma' lift) and T-bars.

The quickest of these is the cable-car. It is usually built to span substantial changes in altitude. There is no technique involved in riding them – the main object is to enter the cabin early enough to get a good view or a position that is least likely to crush you! A location near the front window is a good bet.

Gondolas form the other type of cabin lift but they are much smaller, usually seating four to six skiers. The capacity is multiplied by the number of gondolas on a cable – usually over a hundred. In terms of comfort they are the most pleasant way of ascending the mountain, and in many resorts they form the core of the lift system from which the various chairlifts and draglifts radiate.

Draglifts comprise two main types: T-bars and buttons. T-bars are rare in France but are often seen in Austria and Switzerland. They are anchor-shaped devices on retractable cords and pull two skiers at a time. The key factor with these is to choose a partner of roughly the same height, other-

wise you are likely to end up with the bar either behind your knees or half-way up your back! Before departing, release both hands from the straps on your poles and hold both poles in the outside hand.

Button lifts, or Poma lifts, are easier and more comfortable to ride, which is one reason why they are the normal drag-type installation nowadays. They can also be built to turn corners more easily than T-bars. Most button lifts now feed the pole to you automatically at the departure point. Wait for the gate to open, or the 'traffic signal' to show green, and grab the furthest pole. It will lock on to the

Chairlifts are a comfortable way to ascend mountains quickly and safely

cable and pull you away. Some button lifts take off with a jerk so keep your back loose and relaxed.

Chairlifts are widely used for moving skiers quickly and keeping them at a safe height above the piste. The latest chairs, which sometimes seat as many as four skiers abreast, release from their cable and slow down for an easy departure. Most, however, seat two skiers. To board comfortably, move into position as soon as the previous skiers have been whisked away by the preceding chair.

Learning and progress

Many people take ski lessons for three or four weeks, learn the rudiments of linked parallel turns, and then never take another class. This is a pity because the finer points of skiing, when well instructed, are worth learning if you want to improve. For one thing, skiing, when properly practised, is an easy sport. Those who abstain from ski school invariably pick up the same bad habits – skiing with too much hip and shoulder movement, stiff legs, sitting back and so on.

Taking instruction on artificial slopes can be an excellent way to learn new technique (see Chapter 7).

The slope is short and controlled which makes it an environment conducive to acquiring new skills and ideas. Even more effective for beginners is the latest generation of 'moving mountains' – revolving carpets on which ski technique can be learned rhythmically. The instructor is only feet away from the pupil and can relay instructions calmly, and immediately. On this type of machine you are likely to clock up more mileage in an hour than on any other surface.

In the mountains the best way to learn quickly is to form a group with another two or three skiers and hire a private instructor from the local ski school. He or she will probably enjoy giving the lesson more than teaching a large class and you will gain much more skiing time and individual attention.

If you have a bad experience in ski school, and many people do, do not allow this to deter you. Search out the best instructors and let them work on your technique – the dividends will be enormous.

If you attend ski school beyond an elementary level you will avoid picking up bad habits and enjoy the camaraderie of skiing in a group

Ski safety

As the mountains become more mechanized and better organized there is always the temptation to think that safety is taken care of. This is not the case. A few tips on staying safe while you enjoy your holiday are worth remembering:

1 Look after your body. High-altitude exercise can be strenuous if you spend eleven and a half months of the year at a desk. Apart from undertaking some form of pre-ski conditioning, you should aim to ski gently for the first two days of your holiday. Leave the tougher runs for the second stage of your trip when you will enjoy them more.

2 Watch the elements. Always prepare for the worst even if the sky is pure blue in the morning. Many skiers now use a lightweight backpack for carrying bad weather accessories such as a pair of goggles and a hat. Conversely, watch the sun. Its strength can be formidable, and high-factor sun cream must be applied regularly when skiing later in the season.

3 Avoid collisions. Today's crowded pistes can be hazardous if you stop in the middle of them. Make a habit of avoiding danger by traversing to the side of the piste when stopping. Always look up the hill before skiing away again.

4 Check your bindings. A ski shop can check your bindings cheaply and quickly. Remember to take your boots along. Have this done each year when you have the skis waxed or sharpened.

5 Observe avalanche danger. Avalanches have killed some of the world's greatest mountaineers and skiers, people who thought they knew the risks. And yet, year after year, skiers ignore the dangers and put their lives in jeopardy. Never ski closed runs. Your rescue could endanger rescuers' lives. If you cannot resist the temptation to ski powder when there may be a risk, remember one thing: trees do not grow on avalanche slopes. The existence of mature trees, therefore, indicates less avalanche risk.

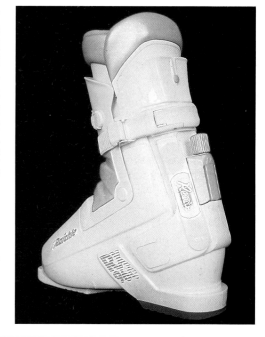

Many mountain rescue teams now rely on the Recco safety device to detect skiers trapped by an avalanche. It is fitted to the back of your boot and reflects the signals transmitted by the Recco detector

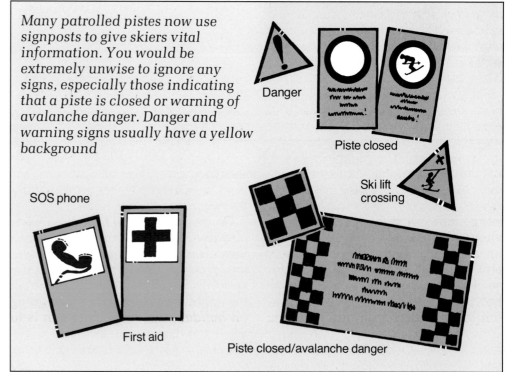

Many patrolled pistes now use signposts to give skiers vital information. You would be extremely unwise to ignore any signs, especially those indicating that a piste is closed or warning of avalanche danger. Danger and warning signs usually have a yellow background

Danger

Piste closed

Ski lift crossing

SOS phone

First aid

Piste closed/avalanche danger

Getting into shape

Sliding down the slippery white slopes actually involves more muscles than you might expect. After the first day getting used to the boards again, your aching body may be screaming out in protest. Ultimately a muscle-flexing fitness fanatic is less likely to feel the strain than an office-bound executive. However, even those enthusiasts who live in the gym might have a few surprises when they get out of bed on the second day, because skiing does actually involve the whole body, in numerous different directions and intensities.

Stories of holidaymakers needing to undertake Olympic training programmes are, generally, grossly exaggerated. Nevertheless, you can benefit from clearing the 'rust' from the system prior to your foray into the icy peaks. But remember that it is a holiday – the mere thought of all that extra hard work beforehand can detract from the prospect of having fun in the snow.

For those who want to be slightly more sporty, without the sweat and tears of an intense physical exercise programme, it is quite easy to wake up the body and the mind before getting on to your skis. In September, when the days are getting noticeably shorter, it is time to start thinking of being more active. For example, when you are going to work, or going out shopping, do not take the escalator or the lift, but use the stairs instead. Then, when you are used to that, try taking the stairs two at a time. Similarly, when you are walking about town, stride out and take longer steps. If you take the bus or tube, you would benefit enormously from get-

Simply increase your usual physical activity to get fit for your holiday

ting off one stop earlier and walking that extra little bit. If you enjoy hitting a ball, just play your game for half an hour longer each week, or try to play twice a week, instead of just once. Your aim should be to increase your sporting activities so that you are working a bit harder without actually thinking about it too much.

Of course you can follow an exercise routine, or join up with an aerobics class. This is a good idea if you are determined to progress in the sport. However, it is important not to lose sight of the fact that you are going on *holiday*, that your chief aim is to enjoy yourself. It is the initial excitement, the relief of escaping from the trials and tribulations of work,

that has the most dangerous effect. The first day never seems quite long enough, and the memory of last year's achievements always surpasses the reality of the eleven-month break. It is always getting out of bed on the second day that puts a damper on the proceedings.

The best way to enjoy your holiday is to take the first day really easy. Stop a bit earlier for tea, and enjoy the Alpine atmosphere over an extended lunch, in the comfort of a mountain restaurant. It is worth spending the extra time checking out all your equipment to make sure that it fits and functions as required. Think ahead, and you will appreciate the mountains as they should be.

Chapter 2 THE BASICS

In all sports, a sound foundation is the cornerstone of improvement, and skiing is no exception. Good skiing starts here: learning how to control your equipment on the nursery slopes and consolidating the basic techniques. Do not make the mistake that some experienced skiers make in thinking that lessons are a tedious way to acquire and practise new skills. The advice in this chapter is designed to complement the teachings of professional ski instructors, for whom there is no substitute. They will teach you not only how to ski well, but also how to enjoy your skiing.

Carrying your skis

Skis are rather awkward things at the best of times, even for advanced skiers. You can often see so-called experienced skiers carrying their skis in the most amusing ways.

Skis are really very easy to carry if it is done properly. The best way is to place the skis together with the bases touching, interlocking at the ski brakes. Then place them over your shoulder with the binding behind the shoulder and the tips facing forwards. Place your hand over the front of the skis in order to balance them. That leaves your other hand free to carry the ski poles. This is very useful, especially when the streets or slopes are icy. You must be careful to remember that this leaves three feet of ski sticking out behind you, which means extra caution is needed when turning around.

There are places where it is not possible to carry your skis in this way – in cablecar queues or in crowded places, for example. The most convenient way to carry them in such places is to grip them above the toe piece of the binding and hold them upright in front of you with the tips facing upwards. If you need both hands to hold your skis, loop the straps of your ski poles over the tips of the skis.

The most efficient way to carry your skis when not in crowded areas is by locking them together and placing them over your shoulder

In busy places, where it would be dangerous to carry your skis over your shoulder, you should hold them upright in front of you

Warm up, loosen up

Even though you may be fit, or have been doing ski exercises, you must warm up before you actually go skiing. Warming up is probably the most neglected area of beginners' and intermediates' skiing. Take time to warm up – if it is good enough for the world's best racers, it is definitely good enough for you.

Not only will a thorough warm-up reduce injury, but it will enhance your enjoyment of the sport and improve your skiing as well. Skiing with cold muscles and poor circulation is like starting your car and putting your foot down on a cold morning. Anyone who knows anything about cars will tell you it will not be long before you have engine damage. Cold muscles and joints slow down your reaction time, thus impairing your co-ordination. Ligaments also lose their elasticity and can tear more easily when cold. So, please try not to ignore the advice on warming up. Get your blood moving and your body ready for a good day's skiing.

Racers always spend time warming up by doing a series of stretching and bending exercises. You too should always limber up, especially after a long chairlift ride, or after lunch or an extended breakfast

Getting used to your skis

There is a left and a right ski. Usually left and right are marked on the ski or there will be an indicator on the bindings. The reason why there is a left and a right ski is that each boot wears down to a different extent and the function of the binding might be impaired if you were to put them on the wrong feet. Also, the inside edges are usually kept sharper.

Choose a flat area for putting on your skis. Place them flat on the snow, with your poles on either side. It is important to check whether any snow is sticking to the heel of your boots – snow on the soles of your boots can prevent them from fitting into the bindings correctly. To clear the snow from your boots, turn your ski pole upside down and hit the sides fairly hard using your pole handle as a hammer. Most of the snow will be removed with the first try. If there is any remaining snow clinging to your boot soles scrape it off on your bindings, or with the ski pole point.

Now, open the heel of your binding and place the boot toe in the front binding piece. Place the heel of your boot over the centre of the heel piece

Use your pole handle to remove snow from your boots before putting on your skis

and push down hard. Repeat with the other ski. To release the bindings, you simply pull up the lever on the heel piece or push down on the heel piece depending on what type of bindings you have.

Skis as an extension of your feet
It is time to move on your skis, but first you must get used to how strange they feel. A good idea is to think of your skis as an extension of your feet. So, start off by trying to become aware of how it feels and where you feel pressure inside your boots when doing the exercises below. You will soon discover that your movement is restricted by your equipment.

Exercises designed to get you used to the feel of your skis will also improve your balance and let you feel the support of your boots. First, lift your ski tips up and down, then pick up each ski in turn and move it to the left and right. Next, using your poles for balance, lean forwards and backwards, then roll your knees to the left and right

Walking on skis

Walking on skis is not very easy at first. You will probably feel clumsy because of your boots and the new extensions of your feet – your skis.

Gliding on one ski first of all will accustom you to the feel and action of walking on skis. Push with one foot and glide on the other ski; try to imagine riding a scooter when you were younger – the action is very similar. Glide for a short distance at first and then increase the gliding distance, using the ski poles and your free leg as balancing aids. After a few tries, put your ski on the other foot and repeat the exercise.

To walk on two skis, stand with your skis hip-width apart. Point them in the direction you want to go, and slide them across the snow. First one and then the other. The movement is similar to walking except that you keep your skis on the snow. When your left ski goes forwards your right arm comes forwards, and vice versa. Your pole should be planted about binding height with the point facing backwards. Throughout this action you should be leaning forwards.

Gliding on one ski (left) is a good exercise for getting used to the feel and action of walking on skis. Cross-country skiing (below) also provides useful experience, since the equipment allows skiers to walk and glide on skis with minimal restriction

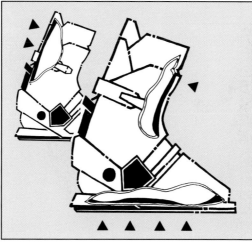

How it feels and where it feels
When you push the left foot forwards, you will feel pressure on the back spoiler of your left boot. The moment you transfer your weight to the left foot, you will feel pressure along the entire length of the foot, and strongly against the left shin, since you must lean forwards as you bring the unweighted right ski forwards. The pressure points will naturally be the same on the right foot as the process is repeated.

Turning around on the flat

Turning around on the flat is quite easy. The method used is called a star turn, which is also an excellent way for first-time skiers to get used to their equipment. The reason it is called a star turn is because the pattern the skis leave in the snow resembles a starburst.

Stepping around the tails
Start off with your skis hip-width apart. Lift the tip of one ski and place it out to the side, keeping the tail of the ski on the snow. Now transfer your weight on to it and lift the tip of the other ski and place it parallel to the first ski. Repeat this until you have turned around. Take small steps to prevent your skis crossing. Your poles should be used for balance.

Stepping around the ski tips
The star turn can be done with a slight variation. Instead of pivoting around your ski tails, you can pivot around your ski tips. Some people find this easier and more natural. It is irrelevant which method you use as the technique is the same.

In stepping around the ski tips, you lift the tail of the ski up and step it sideways, keeping the tip of the ski on the snow. Once again, take small steps, and use your ski poles to help you balance.

The kick turn
There is another way to turn around and this is called a kick turn. However, it is not recommended for novices. It is quite awkward, and can even be dangerous if you have knee or hip problems. Where there are groups of skiers of mixed ability it is safer and better for all to avoid the kick turn altogether.

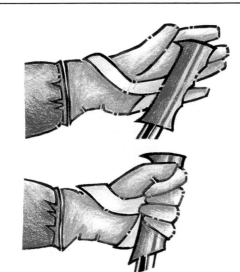

Holding your ski poles
To grip each ski pole put your hand upwards through the strap. With the strap looped around your wrist in this way you will not lose the pole if you fall and let go. Then grip the pole handle with the strap between the thumb and forefinger.

The simplest way to turn around on flat ground is to use the star turn. You can step around either the ski tips (far left) or around the tails (left), whichever feels most natural to you

How it feels and where it feels

When stepping around the ski tails, you should feel your toes hit the top front of your boots, and the heels pressing down as you pick up the front of the ski. When you place the ski in the snow, the pressure will be felt along the length of the whole foot. In stepping around the ski tips, the pressure will be felt along the bottom of your toes and the balls of your feet as the tail of the ski is lifted. Once again, as the ski is placed flat on the snow, pressure will be felt along the length of the whole foot.

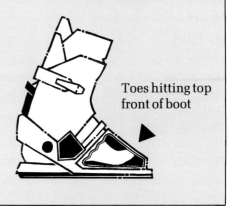

Toes hitting top front of boot

Stepping around the tails

The star turn gets its name from the distinctive pattern left in the snow by the skis as they are stepped around either the tails or the tips

Getting uphill on skis

Before you can ski downhill you must first get up the hill. Similarly, your mobility on the slopes will often depend on your ability to get uphill on skis. It is not as simple as just walking up, since your skis would obviously slide backwards. So how is it done? There are essentially three ways to walk uphill on skis: the herringbone step, the sidestep and the diagonal sidestep.

The herringbone step

This is probably the fastest way to get up an easy slope. Facing uphill, place the ski tips in an open scissor position and push the knees inwards to bring the skis on to their inside edges. The ski poles should be planted behind

When using the herringbone step to climb uphill, you will need to alter your pole grip. Hold your ski pole over the top of the handle, with the thumb and fingers pointing downwards. This will enable you to push off with your poles behind you

The herringbone step takes its name from the pattern left in the snow as you walk uphill. Use it on gentle slopes and short ascents

How it feels and where it feels
When herringboning, the pressure will be felt along the inside of the feet, around the ankle, and on the inside of the shins against the boot tongue. The inner thigh and arm muscles will feel some of the strain of climbing as well. During sidestepping, both straight up the hill and diagonally, the pressure will be felt along the inside of the downhill foot and the outside of the uphill foot as well as around the ankle area.

the body and skis to keep the skis from sliding backwards. In order to do this properly, grasp the poles by placing the palm of the hand on top of the pole grip. Lift one ski and step forwards and sideways and set the ski on its inside edge, transferring your weight on to it. Then simply step the other ski forwards and sideways and repeat the process. A good tip is to take small steps to prevent your skis' tail ends crossing.

The sidestep

First of all, so that the skis do not slide down the hill, you must place them across the fall line – the line that represents the shortest and quickest route down the slope – with your knees and ankles pushed into the hill to put both skis on their uphill edges. Then, step the uphill ski horizontally and sideways, setting it on its uphill edge. Transfer your weight on to it, and lift the downhill ski and place it alongside. Now, put your weight on to the downhill ski and continue this until you are up the hill. Throughout the process the ski poles are used for balance. It is important to make sure that your ankles and knees are pushed into the hill in order for the skis' metal edges to bite.

Once again, small steps will prevent the skis from crossing. If you find that you are sliding backwards or forwards down the hill it is because the skis are not straight across the fall line.

The sidestep is usually used for walking directly up steep hills. Most skiers find it easier than the herringbone step.

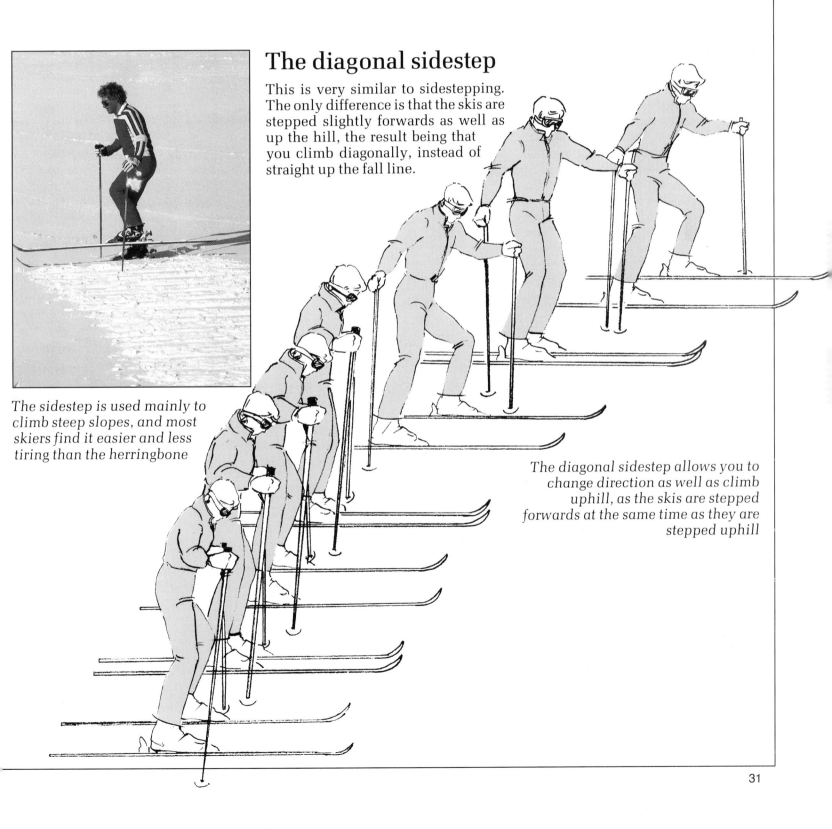

The diagonal sidestep

This is very similar to sidestepping. The only difference is that the skis are stepped slightly forwards as well as up the hill, the result being that you climb diagonally, instead of straight up the fall line.

The sidestep is used mainly to climb steep slopes, and most skiers find it easier and less tiring than the herringbone

The diagonal sidestep allows you to change direction as well as climb uphill, as the skis are stepped forwards at the same time as they are stepped uphill

Matching your skis to the terrain

In order to match your skis and body to the terrain, and to progress as a skier, you are more or less dependent on your ability to feel with your feet, because they are the direct link with your skis. Your feet are not lifeless in your boots, wrapped in a shell of plastic. They are full of small pressure sensors, especially on the soles, which transmit valuable information regarding the pressure along your feet, as well as any changes in pressure that might occur.

It is very difficult in the early stages of learning to ski to be fully aware of this, but the sooner you are able to sense it, the better. It is therefore imperative that your ski boots fit correctly and suit your standard of skiing. It is a good idea to fasten the boot loosely at first until pressure on the soles of your feet can be felt and recognized. After that, buckle the boots up until they fit comfortably and snugly.

Once you become aware that your feet are alive, they will receive and send out all sorts of information regarding the various forces generated by the terrain or turns which will help you stay in good dynamic balance. Dynamic balance is essentially good co-ordination between the balance sensors, nervous system and musculature, and it can be continually improved. Musculature in this context refers to all the muscles that must be continually tensing and relaxing, along with the joints that must also be

bending and stretching to maintain correct balance. Of course, you must also be looking ahead and reading the terrain with your eyes to prepare for any necessary acceleration or braking.

Being aware of the terrain is rather difficult when you first learn to ski, because there are so many other distractions, such as the fear of looking foolish or the fear of what the other people on the slope might think of you. One thing that might help is to remember that most people have enough to worry about without looking at you. In addition, breathing slowly and deeply from your centre will also help. Remember, you can only experience fear if you are breathing as if you were frightened.

Downhill and cross-country racers are always anticipating changes in terrain

Adopting a ready position

A good ready position in skiing is one that allows you to tackle the terrain and cope with turning forces

To cope with acceleration and deceleration of the skis, it is necessary to be in a ready position. However, there is no single correct position for skiing: you are either going into or coming out of a position. In fact, continuous movement is a prerequisite for good skiing. But in order to come and go, you must be ready for motion.

Strange though it may sound, Western films provide a good example of a ready position. It is quite likely that, sooner or later, two cowboys will have a showdown. Take a look at them before they draw their guns — they are in a ready position. Their feet are hip-width apart, they are bent at the ankles, knees and hip joints, and the upper body is slightly forwards, their hands are forwards and out to the side. The natural ready position on skis is similar to that of the cowboys.

In a good ready position for skiing, the feet should be hip-width apart and the weight equally distributed over both feet so that the skis are weighted along their whole length. The skis should be held flat on the snow. The ankles, knees and hip joints should be slightly bent and slightly forwards to compensate for the bend in the lower legs. The arms should be held forwards and out to the side for balance, with the poles pointing behind. The arms are very important and should move within an area in front of the body, and never behind. The head should be held up and looking ahead, not down at the ski tips. From this position you can move vertically or laterally, to the right or to the left.

How it feels and where it feels

You should feel the weight distributed over the entire length of the feet. A little pressure should be felt by the shins against the ski boots, and very little against the boot spoilers. Your toes should be flat. If they are curled, it is a sure indication that you are tense. Tension in any part of the body usually shows up in the neck and upper back muscles. Relax! That is what the ski instructor will probably be saying. Yet, in trying to relax it is quite easy to do the opposite, causing further tension. Instead of trying too hard to relax, stop and take in some of the scenery and slowly breathe some of that fresh mountain air.

How should it feel when you are holding your ski poles? Think of holding a live bird: you must not grip so tightly that it is squashed, nor so loosely that it flies away.

Straight running

To enjoy the sport fully, and continue making progress, you must have a sound knowledge of the basics. What can be more basic than balancing? Most ski instructors are in such a hurry to get their students on the lift that they do not give them enough time to master the basic arts of balancing and gliding. Unfortunately for the student, somewhere along the line this will show up to their disadvantage.

Straight running, or 'schussing', is your chance to try out your ready position. It means sliding straight down the fall line without turning and should be practised again and again. The place to do this is on the nursery slopes. Choose a nice flat run-out with a transition to an incline. With such a slope there is no need to worry about stopping – the incline will bring the skis automatically to a standstill. If the slope has a flat plateau to start from, that is ideal. If not, use your poles to hold you in place before you are ready to start.

Find the ready position and get comfortable. Give yourself a push with your poles if you are on a start plateau, or release the pressure on your poles if you are using them to stop yourself from sliding downhill. What is new is the motion carrying you downhill. You have to guide your skis by holding them parallel; both skis should be travelling in the same direction, not locking your feet and knees together. You do that by adjusting the amount of pressure you have on each ski. Of course, you must also compensate for the acceleration and deceleration of your skis. This is done by flexing and extending vertically

When straight running, always make fine balancing adjustments

from your ready position and altering your body position laterally as well as horizontally.

Remember, skiing is dynamic. To hold the knees bent at a certain angle is just as damaging to your skiing as keeping the legs stiff. The leg and hip joints should be continually bending to make fine balancing adjustments. Sometimes the movements are so minute that they are hardly noticeable. After making a few attempts at straight running you will soon be making all the adjustments necessary to stay in dynamic balance on a moderately flat, even slope, without turning.

How it feels and where it feels
In the beginning there will be a sensation of acceleration; the calf muscles can be felt as they are being pressed against the spoilers at the back of the boot. Naturally, your centre of mass must be shifted forwards. This is done by bending forwards at the ankles, knees and hip joints. Doing this, you can feel the pressure distributed evenly along both feet. In this way, it is possible to feel the slightest variations in the terrain. Then, as you start to slow down, the pressure will be felt against the shins as your body's centre of mass moves forwards.

How to fall

Falling is something beginners and experts have in common, because all skiers fall at one time or another. If you feel as if you are going to fall, try to make a recovery by separating your skis or by whatever means you feel are necessary. If there is no hope of a recovery, accept the fall instead of fighting it.

The most common way to fall is to sit down to one side and bring your skis across the slope. If you are unlucky enough to fall forwards, try to get your skis facing downhill and across the fall line as quickly as possible. At all costs, try to keep your knees out of the snow. Advice about relaxing is often heard, but if you relax too much your knee joint becomes vulnerable. Instead, try to straighten your legs as soon as you get your skis into a position across the fall line.

Avoid attempting to stop by jabbing your ski poles in front of you. Not only do you risk spraining your wrists, but you could end up getting your ski poles literally down your throat.

Knowing how to fall correctly is important to avoid injury. Try to sit to one side, with your arms out in front of you, and straighten your legs as soon as your skis are in position across the fall line

Inertia, gravity and the body's forward momentum all combine to try to tip you over. Maintaining the correct stance with your centre of mass over your skis will help you to stay upright

Getting up after a fall

When you have had some skiing experience you will be able to get up after a fall by simply standing up, provided you are not hurt. However, in the early stages of learning, there is a standard procedure for getting up again. First, you have to get your skis across the fall line. Then, you must bend your knees and pull your skis up underneath you and put them on their edges. You should then place your poles together with one hand on the grips; the other hand should grip the poles near the baskets. The poles should be planted on the uphill side close to you and you should push on them to help you stand up. If you have difficulty, try walking your lower hand up the poles.

An alternative method of getting up depends on you getting in the same position, with your skis pulled up underneath you on their edges and across the hill. This time, both ski poles should be planted uphill close to you. Then, you should push on your poles and stand up. Beginners usually find this way more difficult. Since getting up on skis can be quite difficult at first, take time to get your body into the proper position. Most problems arise when skiers are in too much of a hurry. So, take your time.

With your skis across the fall line, put both poles together and plant them on your uphill side. Grip the handles with one hand and the shafts, just above the baskets, with the other, and push down to lift yourself up

Balancing exercises

To ski well you must exercise to improve your balancing ability; you can do this by moving in and out of the ready position.

1 An excellent exercise is to glide straight down the fall line, while moving your centre of mass forwards then backwards, to discover what happens to your skis.

2 Another exercise is to vary the vertical motion in the legs and upper body. Do this by starting in the ready position, without your ski poles. Sink down and touch the snow with both hands, then extend and reach above your head with both hands while moving.

3 To get used to shifting your weight, lift one ski completely off the snow, and then the other, while gliding down the fall line.

4 Position a friend or practice partner a short distance down the slope, then have him or her throw their glove to you as you schuss past. You, in turn, should attempt to catch the glove and throw it back. This is a fantastic co-ordination exercise.

Most skiers do not do enough of this type of exercise. So, when you are a more proficient skier, use the dullest, most boring stretches of mountain to develop your balancing ability and co-ordination.

It is important not to underestimate the value of balancing exercises. The practice routines shown here are just a few examples of how you can improve your balance and co-ordination

Schussing over bumps

No slope is completely smooth. One of the best ways to learn how to match your skis and body to the terrain for a smooth ride is to ski over a series of equally-spaced man-made bumps, called a wash-board.

These bumps will throw you completely off balance unless you adjust your ready position to enable you to absorb them and go with the terrain. The way to absorb the bumps is to let your legs act as shock absorbers. This is done by flexing forwards in the ankles, knees and hip joints on top of the bumps, and, at the same time, leaning slightly forwards with the upper body to avoid being thrown backwards. Then, extend your legs and upper body down into the trough and get back in the ready position in order to tackle the next bump. Throughout the process your head and upper body should remain relatively still. This movement is similar to that of a car going along on a bumpy road. The body of the car remains level, while the wheels go up and down with the road.

A good tip is to imagine that you are skiing in a tunnel with a low roof and lots of bumps under foot. If you move your body up and down, you will bang your head on the roof of the tunnel. Try to think from the ankles up, so that the bumps are absorbed in the legs, not the upper body. You should also try to keep the skis on the snow, by pushing the ski tips down into the troughs when you extend.

Body movement when schussing over bumps should be restricted to the legs. From the ready position, flex in the leg joints and lean slightly forwards as you go over each bump. Extend down into the trough with your legs and upper body, and adopt the ready position once more to tackle the next bump

The key to absorbing bumps in the terrain is to let your legs act as shock absorbers. Martin Bell of Great Britain allows his knees to come up towards his chest as he schusses down a bumpy downhill course

How it feels and where it feels
When you first approach a bump, you will feel pressure against your shins and on the balls of your feet. On top of the bump you will feel pressure under the arches of the feet. At this point, the skis might cross if you are not careful; that is why you should push the tips down into the troughs. When the skis slide down into the trough, they will suddenly accelerate, creating the sensation that they are slipping away from under you. This will cause pressure against the backs of your boots and under your heels.

Traversing

This is the name given to skiing across a hill without slipping sideways. The technique is also used to connect turns. Your speed is controlled by the line of travel you take; the more you point your skis downhill the faster you will go.

Traversing on flat slopes
The traverse position is best practised initially with your skis hip-width apart. Your ankles, knees and hips should be slightly bent and ready for changes in the terrain. Most of your weight should be on your downhill ski, with both skis on their uphill edges. This is done by pushing your ankles, knees and hips into the hill. The upper body will compensate for this by leaning slightly forwards and over the downhill ski. Your arms should be held forwards and slightly out to the side.

Traversing on steeper slopes
When the slopes are steeper, all these actions must be intensified. Your skis must be put more on edge to achieve greater grip, and your upper body must lean further downhill.

How it feels and where it feels
When traversing you should feel most of the pressure along the inside edge of your downhill foot. Pressure will also be felt around the ankle area and at the top of the shaft of the downhill boot on the inside. Your uphill foot should only feel slight pressure on the outside of the boot.

For traversing flat slopes, adopt a position with open parallel skis. Your body should be bent forwards and downhill at the hips and your knees should be bent into the hill

The exercises below will not only help you with your traversing technique, but they will also help you to improve your angulation and edging

Traversing exercises

The following tips will be useful for improving your traversing. When practising these exercises make sure you do them on both sides, i.e. right *and* left.

1 Start off in a traverse position and ski towards a marked point – for example, a ski pole in the snow or a glove.

2 Try traversing without poles and pushing your downhill knee into the hill with both hands. You will discover that your skis are put on their edges to a much greater extent, and that your upper body faces further downhill, which will improve your angulation.

3 Work on traversing until you leave a clear track in the snow. If you see a track that skids a little, it is a sign that you need more edge on your skis.

4 While traversing, lift your uphill ski off the snow. This guarantees that all your weight is on the downhill ski.

Basic turning steps uphill

This manoeuvre forms the basis of more advanced turning techniques, and is the way in which most skiers perform their first change of direction. More experienced skiers use a variation of these steps to help them ski with independent leg action.

1 Ski straight down an even slope in a ready position.

2 Put your weight on your left ski and pick up your right ski, moving it out slightly to form a 'V' shape with both skis.

3 Now put your right ski down on its uphill edge and transfer your weight on to it, gliding forwards as you bring your left ski parallel.

4 Repeat this, using small steps.

How it feels and where it feels

When you first transfer your weight on to your left foot, you will feel that the sole of your foot has complete contact with your boots from toe to heel. As the right ski is moved out into a 'V', you will feel the pressure move more towards the inside of your left foot. As you transfer the weight on to the right ski you will feel the pressure on the outside of your right foot.

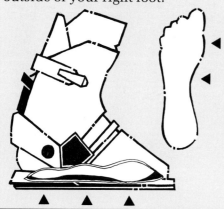

This manoeuvre should also be practised by picking up your left ski. The same sequence should be followed and the pressure points will be the same but in reverse

The snowplough

The snowplough, or the wedge as it is sometimes called, is the basic manoeuvre by which speed is controlled in the early stages of skiing. Snowploughing is very important, since it is here that a great many skiing skills are practised and consolidated. Ask any expert to perform a few snowplough turns, and he is virtually guaranteed to make the same mistakes that he makes in his skiing generally. The most important skills are: turning, edging and pressure.

Women have an advantage when snowploughing because of their physical make-up. They are usually wider at the hips and tend to be a little knock-kneed, which is an advantage. Men usually have smaller hips and tend to be bow-legged, which is a slight disadvantage. Most children get into the snowplough position quite naturally. As we all know, no two people are exactly alike, mentally or physically, so while some of you may find the snowplough manoeuvre quite natural, others may find it quite uncomfortable.

Snowplough stance

Stand on a flat area with your ski tips about hand-width apart and the tails pushed out as far as is comfortable. Your weight should be distributed evenly over both skis. The ankles, knees and hip joints should be slightly bent and your knees should be pointing towards the ski tips. Your upper body should be held forwards to compensate for the bend in the lower legs. Your arms should be relaxed and your hands held forwards and out to the side. The ends of your poles should be pointing behind you. Now, rock backwards and for-

wards on your skis and feel the advantage of having your centre of mass in the middle.

Snowplough glide

Now, step up the hill and glide down the fall line in the snowplough stance. Try to avoid pushing your knees together as your skis will edge too much and cross. If you are making this mistake, you will be feeling that you do not have the strength to push the tails apart and that your leg muscles are overstressed.

Use your practice of the snowplough to develop your turning, edging and pressure skills

How it feels and where it feels
You will feel pressure against your shins and on the balls of your feet. Equal pressure should be felt on both feet.

Regulating your speed in the snowplough

Moving from schuss to snowplough is an important step, one which capitalizes on good dynamic balance and flexing and extending in the legs. When you flex down, pushing your knees towards the ski tips and the tails of your skis apart, you will discover that you start to slow down. This is due to the friction created between the skis and the snow. Try doing this a few times, varying the width of the plough. You can also experiment by pushing your knees further forwards and inwards as you push the tails apart. Further resistance is created in this way since the skis are more on their inside edges, and this, too, will slow you down quite effectively.

Try again by edging the skis more and pushing the tails into a wider plough until you stop. Learning how to slow down and stop in this way often removes fear and this, in turn, increases confidence and greatly facilitates the learning process. Overcoming fear, particularly as a novice, is one of the best ways of improving. (See also Chapter 6.)

Once you know that you can regulate your speed effectively, you will feel more confident on skis. Practise with the width of your plough and with pushing your knees further inwards and forwards

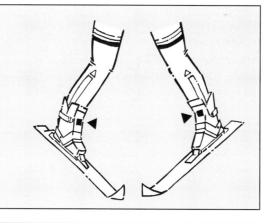

How it feels and where it feels
By flexing in the legs as you push them forwards and inwards, you will feel pressure against your shins. When your edges bite into the snow you will be aware of the pressure under the arches of your feet, as well as a feeling of being on a solid platform. If you feel stiff and restricted in this movement, it might be because you are making too wide a plough.

Improving the pivoting of your skis

You have probably discovered that by pushing your knees forwards and inwards and steering your feet in the direction you want your skis to go, you pivot your skis. Pivoting your skis in opposite directions will give you the snowplough position. If you experiment with the width of your plough you will improve your leg rotation and thus your turning skill.

Practise by starting off in a narrow plough. Then extend in the legs and flex downwards, immediately pushing the tails of your skis apart and your knees forwards and inwards. Extend back into a narrow plough and repeat. It is more or less a bouncing movement – up, down, up, down.

How it feels and where it feels
When you push your skis out into the plough, you will feel equal pressure against both shins and under your big toes as well as the balls of your feet. There will also be a strain on your thigh muscles. The more you edge your skis, the more the pressure will move from the toes to the whole of the inside of your feet. When you extend, you will feel the skis unweight and come into a narrower plough. The wider the plough, the more restricted your movements will be.

Pivoting your skis by experimenting with the width of your plough will improve your leg rotation and turning skill

Snowplough turns

Snowplough turns are probably the way in which you make your first turns on skis. They are also the foundation for more advanced turning techniques. When you are in your basic snowplough stance, you are sure to have noticed that the left ski is pointing to the right and the right ski is pointing to the left, even though you are going straight ahead. This is because your weight is equally distributed between your skis. If you were simply to put more weight on your left ski, you would turn to the right, and vice versa. This is basically how snowplough turns work.

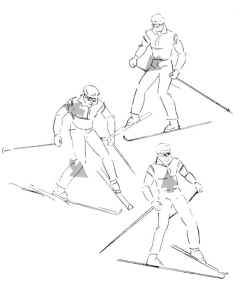

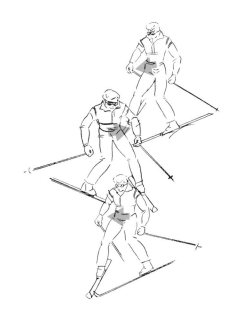

When practising a slight change of direction in the snowplough, try to be aware of your weight change from ski to ski

With a medium change of direction, sink down in the ankles, knees and hips and transfer your weight on to the right ski. Extend, sink down in all three leg joints and transfer your weight on to your left ski

Slight change of direction
Start off on a relatively flat slope in your plough position facing straight down the fall line. Now ski down the fall line and put pressure on your right ski. Do this by bending slightly at the hips over the front of the outer ski. You will change direction towards the left. If you move the pressure to your left ski, you will change direction to the right. This kind of turning is fine if the terrain is flat and you only want to change direction slightly.

Medium change of direction
To effect a medium change of direction, do the same as before, but this time extend in the legs between turns. This vertical motion will give you more pressure control on the turning ski, while flexing in the legs.

Large change of direction
Turning is a more effective way to stop than a snowplough stop. By finishing your turns, you reduce your speed and thus stay in control. Larger direction change can be had when you add leg rotation and foot steering, and vertical motion, to your existing pressure change. Your upper body is counter-rotated slightly when you cross the fall line, which prevents over-turning.

To effect a large change of direction, sink down in all three leg joints and transfer your weight on to your right ski. Drive your knee in the direction you want to go (leg rotation) and extend in all three leg joints

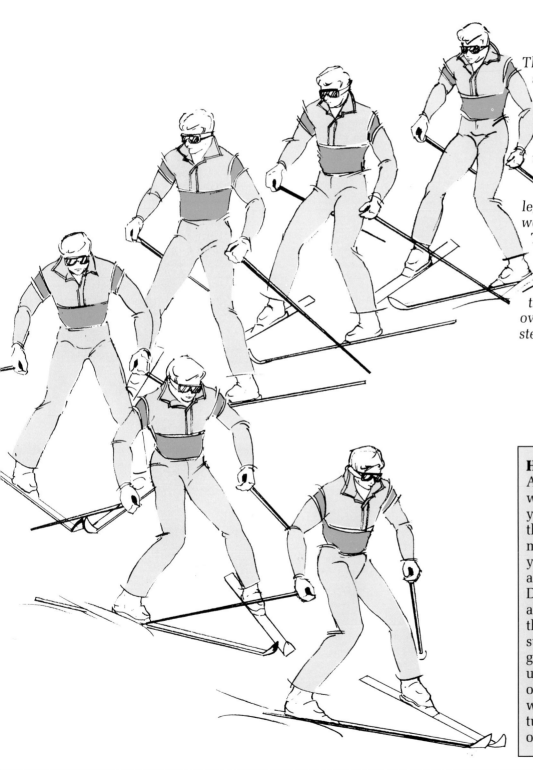

This sequence shows linked snowplough turns with a large change of direction. At the start, the ankles, knees and hips are bent, and the upper body relaxed. The arms are in front and out to the side for balance.

The outside left ski is being pressured and steered round. The legs are then extended and the weight transferred on to the right ski. The knees are pushed forwards and inwards to bring the skis on edge and steer them round. The hips and upper body are held against the direction of travel to prevent oversteering, and the turn is steered out

How it feels and where it feels

As you are steering into a turn, you will feel weight on the whole of your feet. The more you complete the turn, the more the weight will move forwards on to the ball of your outside foot. Pressure will also be felt against your shin. During the second half of the turn, all your weight should be felt on the outside foot. At first, a slight strain will be felt in the hips and groin as you hold your hips and upper body against the direction of travel. With practice, this will improve. At the end of the turn, weight will again be on the outside ski.

47

Sideslipping

Sideslipping is a means of travelling sideways down a slope. It also forms part of a skidded turn, and is useful for controlling your speed on steeper terrain.

To start a sideslip, you should be in a traverse position. There are four ways to initiate a sideslip: stepping downhill, downsinking, downsinking with leg rotation and directing your knees downhill to release your skis' edges. By varying the amount of edging, you control your speed. The flatter your skis are, the faster you will slide. The sideslipping movement is ended by pushing your knees into the hill and bending forwards and sideways at the hips.

Downsinking
Out of the traverse, sink down quickly in the ankles, knees and hip joints. To aid balance, your upper body should make a slight movement forwards and downhill from the hips with your weight over the downhill ski

Stepping downhill
Out of the traverse position, step downhill. Bring the uphill ski together with the downhill ski. Sink down and slide, with your upper body facing slightly downhill and your weight over the downhill ski

Downsinking with leg rotation
Out of the traverse, flex down quickly in all three leg joints and rotate your feet and knees forwards strongly. Direct your knees slightly downhill, with most of your weight on your downhill ski

Sideslipping

How it feels and where it feels

At first, it will be difficult for you to roll your knees downhill to flatten your skis. In fact, you might well be afraid. Your weight should be felt along the arch of your downhill foot. You will have a strong feeling of wanting to use your arms and torso to make your skis slide. This must be avoided. Your upper body should face downhill. By changing the pressure forwards and backwards you will alter the direction of your slide.

Directing your knees downhill
Out of the traverse position, rise up slightly and direct your knees downhill. This will release your ski edges and your skis will slide downhill. It is important to keep your upper body facing downhill with most of your weight on your downhill ski

The stop swing

The stop swing – or emergency stop or hockey stop, as it is also sometimes called – is an extremely useful swing to master. If all skiers were able to do so, there would be far fewer accidents on the slopes.

Rise up out of your ready position, then sink down quickly in all three leg joints while rotating your knees forwards and inwards. Your upper body should be facing downhill. Edge both skis and compensate for this by bending forwards and sideways at the hips

How it feels and where it feels
As you rotate your legs, you will feel pressure on your shins. As your edges grip the snow, you will feel strong pressure along the inside of your downhill foot.

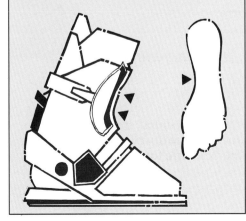

Chapter 3 TECHNIQUE

Skiing is a sport full of challenges. However, many skiers mistakenly believe that progress lies only in being able to tackle successively steeper slopes. They think that because they have good, safe equipment, and can get down today's well-groomed pistes using more or less parallel turns, they have nothing more to learn. They are quite wrong. Real improvement is based on understanding how your skis work and on acquiring and practising those skills that will make your technique reliable in all types of terrain and weather conditions. It is important to realize that the learning process is a continuous one, and should not stop once you can ski red or black runs.

How your skis work

In order to progress beyond an elementary level and to cope with varied terrain and conditions at higher speeds, you must understand something about your skis and how they can work for you.

Skis are precise pieces of engineered equipment designed to work for you when you stand on them correctly. No doubt the majority of skiers have heard of flex, torsional stiffness, camber, reverse camber, and side cut, but do you understand what they mean and the effect each of them has on your skiing? Once you understand how a ski is meant to work, you will stop fighting it and try to work along with it.

Flex

Flex

You have probably tested this for yourself, when you have flexed your skis by hand. The flexion of the ski refers to its bending characteristics. Flex in modern skis varies at different points along the ski; for example, the tail is usually stiffer than the tip. In the past, it used to be said that a good ice ski was one with extremely stiff flex. Nowadays, because of the modern materials used in ski manufacture, that is no longer the case. A ski can have a moderately soft flex, and still hold well on ice, because the ski's flex works hand in hand with its torsional stiffness.

Reverse camber

Reverse camber is what happens when you compress the ski more than flat. All skis need to be put into reverse camber in order to carve. Reverse camber works together with the side cut of the ski.

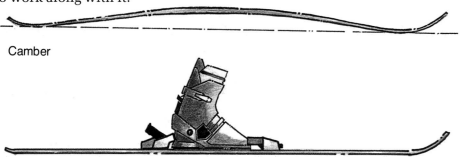

Camber

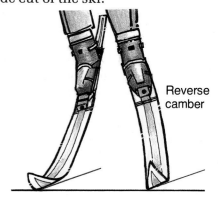

Reverse camber

Camber

If you place a ski on an even surface you will notice that it is not exactly flat, and that it has a slight arched shape – this is known as the camber. Without camber your skis would only bite into the snow at the middle, leaving the tip and tail without snow contact. So, the function of camber, as it has been expressed many times before, is to distribute the skier's weight evenly along the running surface (the base) of the ski.

Side cut enables racers to carve turns at maximum speeds. Peter Mueller of Switzerland rides the inside edge of his outside ski to turn down a steep downhill course

Side cut

This refers to the shape of the ski. For example, it is wider at the tip and the tail than in the mid-section, or waist. This allows the ski to carve an even arc through the snow when put in reverse camber and rolled on edge. To help you understand a little more clearly, place the ski on a flat surface. Make sure the ski stoppers are out of the way. Now tilt the ski on edge. You will notice that only the tip and the tail are in contact with the surface. What happens if you now apply pressure to the binding area? The result is that the whole edge makes contact with the surface. Now, tilt the ski even more on edge, until you can push down on it to get reverse camber. Notice the arc the ski's edges form when you roll it on edge and bend it.

Torsional stiffness

Torsional stiffness refers to the ski's ability to twist along its length, and determines how well the ski follows the terrain during carved turns. Imagine a ski that is extremely soft (easy to twist) torsionally: each time you roll the ski on edge, the tip and tail will remain relatively flat on the snow, not providing the necessary edge bite to carve a turn. By contrast, a ski that is too stiff torsionally would continually hook at the tip. Most modern skis are designed so that they are continually twisting and untwisting during skiing in order to follow the terrain.

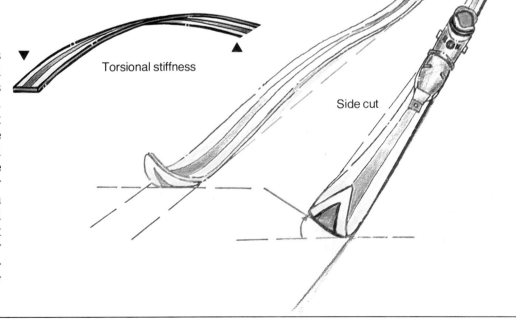

Torsional stiffness

Side cut

Steering your skis

Once you are clear about how your skis work, the next step is to look at the various ways of steering them.

Recently there has been a lot of discussion about carving turns. It is important to realize that carving alone is not the answer, neither is skidding. You need them both. When the situation changes you need to be able to alter your steering to meet the conditions. From beginner to good parallel skier, turns are steered primarily by skidding, and a combination of skidding and carving. For more advanced skiers and racers carving turns becomes their goal.

There are essentially four ways to steer your skis:

Gerissenes steering

The word gerissen is German in origin and has historical roots (*Gerissener Kristiania*). Today this type of steering is only seen in the stop swing.

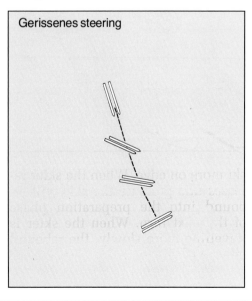

Gerissenes steering

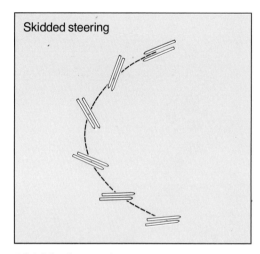

Skidded steering

Skidded steering

Skidded steering is used mainly by beginners and skiers of intermediate level. When the skis turn they slide sideways and downhill, across their edges, losing height and causing the skis to brake.

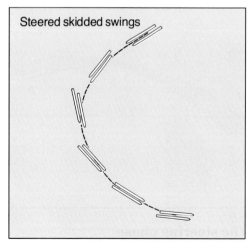

Steered skidded swings

Steered skidded swings

This type of steering is used by more advanced skiers and experts. Steered skidded swings make it possible to steer your skis on hard or steep slopes, without losing a lot of height.

The tracks left in the snow by a carved turn with minimal skidding

Carved swings

The goal of carving turns is to complete the turns with minimal braking effect. Therefore, the skis must skid sideways as little as possible. In other words, the tails of your skis should pass along and through the same line as the tips. These turns are usually attempted by expert skiers and racers.

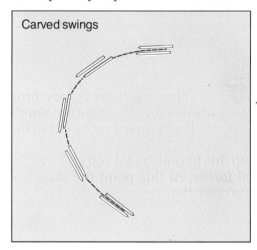

Carved swings

The three phases of a turn

Although you should think of turning as a flowing, continuous movement, a turn in fact has three phases: the preparation phase, the initiation phase, and the steering phase. Try not to think of one part of a turn as being more important than another or holding the secret to great skiing by itself. All three phases merge into one. It is the turn as a whole that connects to the next. Even with this small piece of information you might better understand picture sequences of skiers in action, and ski with a little more feeling.

The preparation phase
This is the part of the turn where most happens. In this phase the skis are unweighted and are 'skimming' over the snow. The skier's centre of mass crosses over the skis towards the inside of the new turn, causing the skis to roll through flat on to their new edges. The skier also moves his weight on to the new outside ski and starts the steering of the skis into the new turn.

The initiation phase
The skier moves into the fall line and keeps the turn flowing onwards by steering the skis with his feet and legs. At this stage there is very little pressure on the skis except the skier's weight. The skis now move out of the fall line and pressure starts to build up due to centrifugal and gravitational forces. At this point the skier can increase the pressure on the skis himself. If so, this must be done gradually so that the skis are pressured fully in the steering phase.

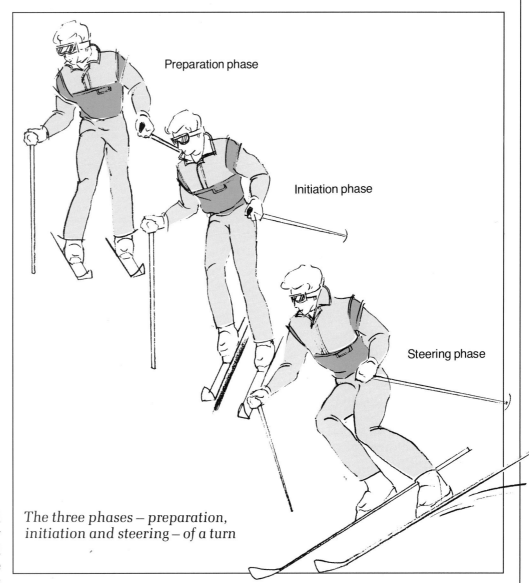

Preparation phase

Initiation phase

Steering phase

The three phases – preparation, initiation and steering – of a turn

The steering phase
This is the phase of the turn where the edged outside ski is fully pressured and seems to turn with no effort. This pressure builds up until the end of the steering phase when it should be at its greatest. If necessary, this can be brought about by putting the outside ski more on edge. When the skier releases this pressure the skis will rebound into the preparation phase of the next turn. When the skier is travelling more slowly, the rebound effect will be less, and the process can be helped by more pronounced vertical motion.

Turning your skis

With your knowledge of how skis work, the different types of steering available and the different phases of a turn, you should now consider the role of the following three important skiing skills: turning, edging and pressure.

Turning the skis means that you are changing the direction in which they are travelling. Skiers try to do this by rotating their legs either simultaneously or independently. Your legs rotate in their hip sockets, but they can only do this effectively if you adopt a good ready position which allows them to do this. Of course you can turn your skis by rotating your upper body, but that is neither functional nor effective in skiing. Most of the time skiers turn their skis independently. Because of our physical make-up we are used to independent leg action – in walking, riding a bicycle, ice skating and so on – and all two-legged motion has to be learned. In skiing terms you must be careful not to confuse turning that looks as though the skis are turning at the same time and turning with the legs together. Remember, all movement in skiing can be so subtle that it is hardly noticeable.

Rob Boyd of Canada edges his skis to turn in the downhill

Edging

This is the way in which you will adjust your ski's base so that it is at an angle to the snow. As we have already seen in the section on how a ski works, edging is necessary for all types of turning. The degree to which you tip your skis on edge in a turn is dependent on many factors. Remember, though, that there is no one correct amount of edge angle for turning since this is continually changing.

Angulation

The way you edge your skis is closely related to angulation. Angulation is simply bending forwards at the hips, while your legs are bending forwards and inwards to edge the skis thus allowing pressure to be applied to the inside edge of your outside ski.

By angulating correctly, you can achieve the advantage of greater edging. However, angulation is not something that can be learned in a static position; it is constantly changing. Therefore, there is no one correct angulated position, just as there is no one correct balance position.

There are in fact three ways to angulate: knee angulation, hip angulation and knee-hip angulation. All three types of angulation should occur naturally and should not be executed with a contorted or exaggerated body position. Remember, angulation is a natural movement that helps you remain in good dynamic balance.

Knee angulation
This type of angulation is the quickest. It is usually used for turns close to the fall line.

Hip angulation
When the skis are turned more out of the fall line, and higher speeds are reached, hip angulation is necessary.

Knee and hip angulation
This is the type of angulation used by most racers, depending on the situation. With it the outside ski can be kept on a higher edge.

Flexion and extension
This is a very important aspect in skiing and goes hand in hand with turning your skis. Again, because of the way we are built, it is very difficult to rotate the legs when standing upright. Therefore, try extending in between the turns, and flexing while rotating the legs in the initiation and steering phases of the turn.

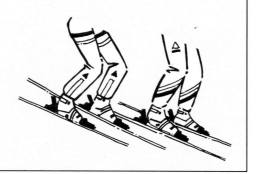

Knee angulation (below); Vreni Schneider of Switzerland demonstrates hip angulation (below right), and Pirmin Zurbriggen, also of Switzerland, the racers' extreme form of knee and hip angulation

Pressure

Pressure is necessary for steering your skis. This pressure, which is between the snow and the skis, can be increased and changed forwards and backwards.

To increase the pressure, simply pick up one ski. In doing this you will have increased the pressure on the other ski. The pressure can also be increased by tipping both skis on edge or tipping one ski on edge and picking up the other.

By altering the pressure forwards and backwards you will affect the way the ski behaves. If you apply pressure to the front of the ski's edges to bite into the snow, the ski tips will go uphill, causing the turn to tighten and slow you down. Pressure applied to the tails of the skis will cause the arc of the turn to lengthen and the skis to accelerate.

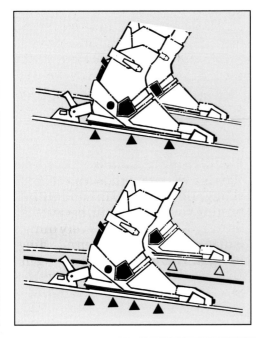

The basic swing

The basic swing is an excellent way to practise the three skills turning, edging and pressure as one and incorporated into swings. It will also enable you to get out on the various lifts and put some miles under your skis.

The basic swing is a combination of those manoeuvres you will already have practised many times: traversing, snowploughing and sideslipping. In addition to these, you will need to use your pole plant, which may at this stage be unfamiliar to you. Try putting all four actions together as follows:

1 Start off in a traverse ready position with your skis hip-width apart.
2 Flex down in the leg joints and put your skis into a plough. At first push both skis into a plough, then step out the uphill ski. The sooner you can do this the better.
3 Now make a few turns, ending each with a traverse.

4 Do the same as before but bring the inside ski towards the downhill ski sooner. Keep trying to close the inside ski towards the outside ski sooner until you are doing this in the fall line. At this point it is time to use your pole. An exercise to help get the timing and feeling for the pole plant is the plough swing or plough christie.

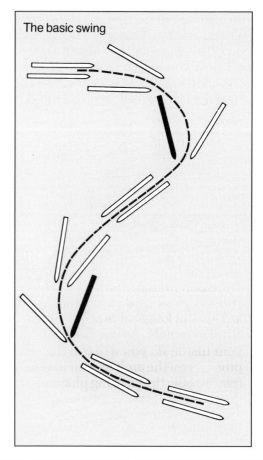

The basic swing

The plough swing
Start off in your plough position, then sink down in all three leg joints and prepare for the pole plant. Stop this downsinking suddenly, plant your pole and immediately push up from the inside edge of your inside ski while extending. Bring the inside ski towards the outside ski and flex down in all three leg joints while steering your skis. Your upper body should compensate for the forces produced by bending forwards and sideways at the hips (angulation)

The basic swing with uphill stem

When you attempt the basic swing with an uphill stem you will need to combine what you have practised so far. It is far better to practise several swings, one after the other, instead of one swing at a time:

1 You should approach the turn in a ready position in the traverse.

2 Flex down slightly, put your outside ski more on edge and stem the inside ski out into a plough position.

3 Now, pressure the new outside ski slightly so that you enter into the fall line.

4 Flex down further in the ankles, knees and hip joints, and then stop this suddenly. Flex down further in the ankles, knees and hip joints. At the same time prepare to plant your pole. Plant your pole and stop the down flexing suddenly. Extend up from the inside edge of your inside ski.

5 Bring the inside ski closer to the outside ski and steer out the turn by flexing down in the leg joints and rotating your legs in the direction you want to go. A slight holding back of the outside hip with angulation is necessary.

When practising the basic swing with uphill stem, try linking several swings together to gain the full benefit of the exercise

How it feels and where it feels
When the skis come into the fall line you must adjust for the acceleration. You will then feel increased pressure against your shins as you sink down in the ankles and knees in preparation to plant your pole. As you push off your inside ski you will feel the pressure on the arch of your inside foot. During the steering phase of the swing more pressure should be felt on the outside foot and against both shins.

The uphill stem

The uphill stem is a modern innovation associated with 'sporty' skiing, and it does have several advantages. Many skiers feel uneasy at the moment their skis pass through the fall line. However, the stemming out motion allows you to maintain constant control over your skis because you actually step into the fall line. This helps you build confidence and stability. Also, as you step on to the new outside ski you achieve a much better feeling for the new direction of travel. A further advantage is that the change from edge to edge becomes much easier.

Uphill stem swings differ from basic swings in two ways. First, the unweighting and changing of edges and pressure occurs before the fall line, not in the fall line. Second, the steering phase of the turn must be improved so that less skidding takes place. You might also want to get your skis a little closer but that should happen naturally so do not try to push them together.

Changing basic swings into stem swings

Now that you have practised and gained experience of the basic swing, it is time to change it into a more 'sporty' way of skiing – the stem swing. You already know what has to be changed so once again it is simply a question of practice.

Begin by making some basic swings, and keep trying to extend and close the skis earlier. In order to improve your steering, try some swings to the hill.

The uphill stem
Start off in a traverse in your ready position. Pick up the inside ski and stem it out, placing it on the new inside edge. At the same time as your pole is planted, extend forwards and upwards from the inside edge of the outside ski. Bring the inside ski towards the outside ski and steer the turn out using leg rotation, angulation and holding the hips against the direction of the turn

The uphill stem viewed from behind

Turning and extending

In the initiation phase of the turn, the skis are turned at the same time as they are unweighted. This happens as one movement. It is done by extending forwards downhill. If you can accomplish this you will make turn initiation much easier. The same applies in the case of step swings and parallel swings.

How it feels and where it feels

As you stem out the inside ski you will feel pressure on the inside edge of your outside foot as well as around the inside ankle area and the inside top of the boot shaft. This is because the inside edge of the outside ski is pressured very strongly. When you transfer the pressure to the new outside ski you should feel a slow build up of pressure as your skis start to enter the fall line and then travel out of the fall line.

Swings to the hill

Start off in an upright position, then sink down in the ankles, knees and hip joints, driving your knees inwards and in the direction you want to go. Your upper body should angulate to compensate for the forces created on your skis. Remember, your outside ski should be pressured much more than the inside one. This will allow the inside ski to come closer to the outside ski. Keep steering your skis until the tips face uphill

Parallel open stepped swings

When reference is made to stepped turns this means quite simply stepping from one ski to the other. You can either step downhill, step uphill, or scissor.

From the uphill stem it is quite an easy jump to parallel open stepped swings. The only difference is that the inside ski is stepped out and placed on the snow parallel to the outside ski, instead of being placed in a stem position.

In the beginning you might find it hard to initiate your turns without a stem. If so, build up gradually, decreasing the width of your stem until you are stepping out parallel. It is also important to concentrate on extending and turning at the same time.

How it feels and where it feels
The feeling and pressure are the same as in the uphill stem. The only difference is that the inside ski is stepped out parallel instead of in a stem. For this reason you might need a stronger extension forwards and upwards.

In this sequence, the parallel open stepped swing is seen from the front and from behind

Parallel swings with up unweighting

Parallel swings or turns are the ultimate dream of many skiers, and some even believe skiing stops here. In fact, it only starts here. That may sound a little far-fetched, but the fact is that parallel swings are not the be all and end all. Skiing has many variables, and there is no definitive swing for all conditions.

However, parallel swings can easily be varied, and they lend themselves to a variety of terrain and snow conditions. In addition, parallel swings make for very elegant skiing, either with opened or closed skis. There are many ways to initiate parallel turns, but the most common is up unweighting with vertical motion.

The only difference between parallel swinging and stem and step swinging is that in parallel turning the skis do, as you would imagine, actually remain parallel all the time. There is no stemming and both skis are unweighted and turned at the same time. Apart from this, the steering phase is the same as in stem swings and stepped swings – a mixture of skidding and carving.

You will almost certainly find parallel swings easier in the beginning if you use an open stance. Later, when your balance is finer, you will be able to close up your skis. You must concentrate on extending forwards and downhill, while turning your skis at the same time.

The stem swing (below left) and parallel swing (below) from behind

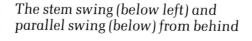

Approach your turning point in a ready position, then flex down in the ankles, knees and hip joints while preparing to plant your pole. Plant your pole and extend forwards, upwards and downhill from both skis. Rotate your legs in the direction of travel, while edging the skis by flexing down in the three leg joints and pushing your knees into the hill. You should angulate with your upper body. Steer the skis out in the same way as for stem and stepped swings

How it feels and where it feels
When you prepare to plant your pole you will feel pressure on both shins as you sink down in the legs. As you extend forwards downhill you should have the feeling that the skis are turning at exactly the same time. During the steering phase pressure will be felt along the arch of the outside foot and outside edge of the inside foot. However, more pressure should be felt on the downhill foot. Pressure will also be felt against both shins.

Short swings

Short swings often give rise to a few problems initially. First, you must stay in the fall line. This might make you a little apprehensive, but with practice you will soon become confident. The dynamics of the swings are very different from those you have already experienced, and you will need to have quick reactions.

Short swings involve the same technique as parallel turns; only the action is different. The flexing and extending in the legs and the edge set are intensified. The frequency of the swings is also increased.

Tracks in snow left by short swings

How it feels and where it feels
The pressure felt here is almost exactly the same as in parallel swings with up unweighting. The only difference is that the pressure will be felt much more quickly and will be more intense.

Short swings must be performed in the fall line, and rhythm and co-ordination are the crucial elements

Carving

Carving, or balancing on the inside edge of the outside ski throughout the turns, is what most racers try to achieve. Carving is not new, yet it is only in the last few years that the recreational skier has become aware of its advantages. However, you cannot learn how to carve without knowing what it feels like. Here are a few exercises designed to help you understand how a ski can work for you, and to give you an idea of how a carved turn should feel. You might find it useful at this point to look once again at the section on how your skis can work for you.

Find a nice easy slope, preferably one with few people and a quick lift service. Start out in your basic ready position. Let your skis run straight down the fall line, and then push one of your knees inwards, in order to put your ski on edge. Do not apply any rotation of the leg, feet, hips or upper body; simply remain balanced over the edge of your ski. Keep the pressure on it until it starts to turn. Maintain this pressure until you want to change direction, then simply roll your other knee inwards and move the pressure on to your new outside ski. Remember, no rotational forces should be applied, since this will cause the skis to slip sideways. After you have made a few changes of direction, stop and look back at your tracks in the snow. If they look similar to the ones shown you have been successfully carving turns.

A variation on this exercise is to experiment in order to find out at what point you apply the pressure. First, try applying pressure to the ball of your foot, then the whole of your

foot and finally the heel. Keep trying this until you can feel the difference in the radius of the turns.

Finally, a good exercise is to experiment with the edge angle in relation to the snow. Tilt your skis more on edge throughout the turns and discover the difference it makes to the radius of the turns.

While practising these exercises you may have discovered that the more forward pressure you apply and the more edge angle, the tighter the radius of the turn will be. You might also have discovered that, at the beginning of the turn, it is better to weight the ball of the foot, changing the pressure towards the heel at the end of the turn.

Now, try to incorporate this feeling into your everyday skiing. The fact that you know what a carved turn should feel like will help you minimize the skidding in your swings.

A carved turn (above) and the track it leaves in the snow (above left). Carving turns will help minimize the skidding in your swings

There are two golden rules to bear in mind when incorporating this into your skiing: first, edge your ski; then, second, pressure it. Skiing is essentially very simple. Just remain balanced over the inside edge of your outside ski while swinging.

How it feels and where it feels
When carving swings you will feel extreme pressure along the arch of the outside foot, and around the inside shaft of the outside boot. The inside ski is usually off the snow or just skimming over it. Therefore, little pressure should be felt on the inside foot.

What many skiers do not realize is that they are very often practising the faults and bad habits they acquired as soon as they stopped taking regular lessons from a qualified ski instructor. This can be extremely frustrating for skiers who are eager to tackle increasingly difficult runs but who are unable to make significant progress. Most common skiing faults can be put right very quickly. The problem lies in recognizing them. This chapter identifies those errors seen every day in the mountains and shows you how to cure them and improve your confidence and skiing ability.

Ski tips crossing in the snowplough

The main reason why skis cross when snowploughing is the tendency of some skiers to sit back. This causes the tips to become light and cross easily. To overcome this problem, try to imagine that you have a tomato in the front of each of your boots. Your aim is to squash them with your shins and to do this your weight must be well forwards.

Your skis will also cross if you push your knees together. This brings both skis on to their edges and, because they are travelling straight ahead but in opposite directions, they will inevitably cross over. By pushing your knees together you limit your ability to rotate your legs and push the ski tails outwards. To prevent this happening, push your knees towards the ski tips instead of together.

How it feels and where it feels
If you are sitting back, you will feel a strain on your thigh muscles. When you snowplough for longer distances in this position you will get a burning sensation in your thighs. If you are pushing your knees together you will have the feeling that you are unable to push the ski tails apart and, once again, your thigh muscles will be stressed. For the correct feeling, see the section on the snowplough glide in Chapter 2.

Sitting back is probably the most common reason for ski tips crossing in the snowplough

In the correct snowplough position (above), your weight should be evenly distributed over both skis

Pushing your knees together will also cause your ski tips to cross. Avoid this by pushing your knees towards the ski tips

The stiff outside leg syndrome

This problem usually arises when beginners start to learn how to perform snowplough turns. It also happens when more experienced skiers attempt to ski terrain that is difficult for them. When there is no motion in the ankles, knees and hip joints, the upper body tends to turn in the direction you want to go. This is to assist the turning of the skis and creates an additional related problem. The rotating of the torso usually causes the outside leg to go stiff and the weight to shift to the uphill ski.

A way to overcome this problem is to ski with more independent leg action. Try lifting the inside ski off the snow when you start your turns. This will increase the flexibility in the lower leg.

An alternative method is to number the degree of ankle flex you achieve during the turn. Number 1 would

denote stiff-legged, 2 bending a little and 3 bending until you can go no further. Try to be aware of which number you reached when flexing. Also, try copying skiers who ski with loose, flexible leg movements.

If you are skiing with a stiff outside leg (left), it will feel generally uncomfortable and you will find it difficult to turn your skis. Skiing with independent leg action will help you flex correctly in the ankles (bottom left)

How it feels and where it feels
If you are skiing with a stiff lower leg, you will have the feeling that your skis do not want to turn. In addition, all the muscles in your lower leg will be strained. You might even think you have weight on your downhill ski, but what you are actually feeling is the resistance of the downhill ski on the snow.

When flexing correctly in the ankles, you will feel pressure along the inside of your downhill foot and on the shins. At the same time, pressure will be felt around the inside of the ankle of the downhill leg and at the top of the inside boot shaft.

Inability to hold a traverse

The traverse is an important manoeuvre because most of the time when skiing you will either be coming out of a traverse or going into one. The rest of the time you will be in the fall line.

The main reason why some skiers have trouble holding a traverse is because they lean into the hill and twist the downhill shoulder and arm forwards, causing their weight to shift to the inside ski. This, in turn, causes the downhill ski to slip away. In addition, the inability to roll your ankles, knees and hips into the hill will cause the skis to remain flat, making them slide sideways downhill instead of gripping the snow.

If you find that you have developed these faults, try putting both hands on the downhill knee while traversing and pushing your downhill knee into the hill (see also Chapter 2).

How it feels and where it feels

If you are committing any of these errors, it will feel as though you are fighting to stay in the traverse position. When it all comes together, you will experience strong pressure under the arch of your downhill foot and around the ankle area, as well as at the top of the inside boot shaft.

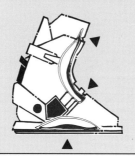

If your downhill ski slips away in the traverse (above left), you are probably leaning into the hill, causing your weight to shift to the inside ski. A better traverse position (above) is one in which the skis are edged slightly by rolling ankles, knees and hips into the hill

Pushing your downhill knee into the hill while traversing is a good exercise for improving edging

Are you too static?

Most recreational skiers seem to think it is fashionable to ski with as little motion as possible. The majority of these skiers look like statues, more akin to something you would find in a wax museum than on a ski slope. In fact, if you look around you on the slopes, most skiers seem to ski from position to position with no motion whatsoever. The next time you watch world-class ski racing on the TV, particularly slalom or giant slalom, you will notice how all racers use natural vertical motion in the ankles, knees and hip joints, regardless of the country they come from. For good efficient skiing, it is necessary to extend between turns. This extension does not have to be demonstrative, just functional.

This constant vertical motion, or up and down motion, serves a number of purposes:

1 Sometimes it is needed on bumpy terrain to keep the skis in contact with the snow. (Like the wash-board exercise in Chapter 2.)
2 On smoother terrain, it helps you turn by unweighting your skis when the up motion is stopped.
3 Vertical motion helps bring your centre of mass to the inside of the next turn.
4 It gives tired leg muscles a chance to rest.
5 The up and down motion assists angulation and helps you pressure your skis more.

This is not to advocate that you should jump around the hill like a kangaroo. How much vertical motion you should use depends on the ter-

Static skiing (above) automatically impedes flexible movement. More efficient skiing (above right) requires extension between turns

rain, snow, and speed at which you are travelling. However, try to bear in mind that it should not be your aim to ski as if you are posing for the front cover of a ski magazine.

If you are trying to make the leap to the advanced level by doing less, try the flying parallel turn. This is in fact a normal parallel turn but the skis are unweighted so strongly and quickly that they are lifted completely off the snow and turned in the air. Try executing this without losing your balance during the takeoff or landing. It will definitely put you on the road to more dynamic skiing.

How it feels and where it feels
If you are skiing statically, you will feel very stiff. It will also seem as though a lot of effort is needed to turn your skis. When you apply vertical motion you should feel pressure against your shins and along the length of your feet before you extend. When you extend, turn your skis at the same time, then sink back down to steer the skis out.

Losing your balance in the fall line

Many skiers find it difficult to get used to the acceleration of their skis when they come into the fall line. You must remember that as soon as your skis hit the fall line they are going to accelerate. Do not worry! You will slow down as soon as your skis no longer point directly downhill. If you find that you panic as your skis accelerate in the fall line, it is probably because you have been caught sitting back on your ski tails. Try to compensate for this accelerating force by bringing your centre of mass over your skis as you come into the fall line. Think back to the basics and to how you continually adjusted your position when straight running over the wash-board.

You will lose your balance in the fall line if you are caught on your ski tails (above left). Try bringing your centre of mass over your skis to compensate (above)

Lack of rhythm

The outcome of lack of rhythm is the inability to link up turns fluently. Skiing is a dynamic sport with continuous movement, yet when you look around the slopes, you might not think so. Rhythm and flow are essential for good skiing.

The reason why many skiers have a problem linking their turns together is because they make long traverses in between. They do not see the turns as one movement, but rather as many separate technical parts; they move from one part to the next, instead of trying to achieve a feeling of rhythm. Try to make the end of one turn flow into the beginning of the next.

There are many ways to inject rhythm and flow into your skiing. One of the best ways is to sing or hum an appropriate tune. Talking yourself through the turns also helps – uup, dowwwn, uup, dowwwn. Alternatively, you could try exhaling throughout the steering phase of the turn. As you do so, breathe out with a whistling sound.

How it feels and where it feels
If your turns are not fluid you will know. When you have improved your rhythm, you will experience a yielding in the legs as you flow from one turn to the next.

How it feels and where it feels
If you are caught on the tails of your skis in the fall line, you are going to feel pressure against your spoilers and your heels. If you are standing in the middle of your skis, you will feel the pressure distributed along the whole length of your feet.

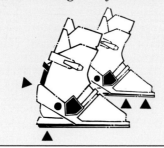

Leaning into the hill with your body

The result of leaning into the hill with your body is that you can apply little or no weight to the downhill ski. This can also happen when you rotate your upper body and hips faster and in the same direction as your skis. Leaning into the hill with the whole body is called banking, and is the method used by skiers to counteract centrifugal force. When there is too much banking, your weight will go on to your inside ski. In order to compensate for this, you must angulate. Just how much angulation you need to keep in good dynamic balance depends on how fast you are going, the pitch of the slope and the radius of the turns.

Too much banking will cause your weight to go on to your inside ski

To check that you are balancing on the inside edge of your outside ski make nice round turns, while picking up the inside ski. It is impossible to pick up the inside ski if you are not standing fully on the outside ski. If you stand on one ski instead of two, you double the weight on that ski. Therefore, you have doubled the force available to flex the outside ski. When you are standing on your skis correctly, they will turn because of the way they have been constructed. This is vital when skiing in icy conditions and is why world-class racers are constantly striving to stay over the inside edge of their outside ski in the steering phase of their turn.

Proper angulation will ensure that you are balancing on the inside edge of your outside ski

A good exercise is to pick up the inside ski while turning – to do this your weight must be on the outside ski

How it feels and where it feels
If you are standing with too much weight on the inside ski, you will feel the skis washing-out or skidding sideways down the hill. When you are balanced correctly on the inside edge of the outside ski it will give a very different and secure feeling – a forwards-onwards motion. Pressure will be felt along the arch of the outside foot and around the ankle area, and at the top of the boot shaft.

The wash-out of the downhill ski

The wash-out of the downhill ski is also known as 'abstem' and is usually caused by rotation. Rotation means that your upper body and torso are travelling faster than, and in the same direction as, your skis. It restricts your ability to angulate and this in turn makes it difficult for you to edge your skis sufficiently, thus resulting in the downhill ski skidding sideways, or washing-out.

If you are not sure whether you are committing this error, there is a simple way to check. Ski a few runs on a nice easy slope holding your ski poles out in front of you. Make sure the poles are facing slightly downhill. If you are turning your upper body and torso faster than your skis, you will become aware that the poles are no longer pointing downhill.

Your downhill ski will skid away if you rotate your upper body

To prevent the downhill ski washing-out, you need to angulate (above). Use the javelin turn (below) as an exercise to prevent rotation

How it feels and where it feels
If you are committing this error, it will feel as though your weight is on the downhill ski, when it is really on the uphill ski. The reason for this is that you will receive strong resistance from the downhill ski when it stems out. If you are steering correctly you will have a sort of forwards-onwards flow with strong pressure under the arch, around the ankle area and at the top of the boot shaft of the downhill foot.

A good exercise to help remedy this problem is to perform some javelin turns. Start off on a nice easy slope, making any kind of turn that you wish. Then lift the uphill ski and cross it over the downhill ski during the steering phase of the turn. It is important that you keep the tip of the uphill ski facing down towards the snow. This helps bring the upper body into a good steering position. Now try to rotate your hips forwards without uncrossing the skis. It is impossible.

Looking down at your skis

Looking down at your skis is a very common error. Your skiing will probably not be affected by the occasional look, but you should certainly avoid watching them all the time. If you keep looking down at your skis, your field of vision will be reduced and you will be unable to read the terrain ahead. It also tends to put you in a rather square position over your skis, preventing good reaction ability and therefore good dynamic skiing.

As a solution to this problem, try looking ahead and keeping the muscles around your neck and shoulders loose. This will increase your field of vision and make it easier to read the terrain; it also allows the continuous freedom of movement that is necessary for good skiing.

Looking down (above left) prevents dynamic skiing – look ahead instead

Controlling your speed

Controlling speed is a problem that afflicts skiers of all abilities. For beginners it is usually tied up with the problems associated with snowploughing. At a more advanced level, it can be the result of plain recklessness. However, most of the time it is due to a lack of simple basic skills, like pivoting and edging. If you have this problem and you ski steep slopes, the outcome can be hazardous. The steepness of the slopes intensifies the acceleration of the skis. What you need here is the ability to link short flowing swings with a good edge set at the end of each turn. It is important that you finish your turns.

An excellent way to improve your pivoting and edging ability is by practising the following exercise.

Find a partner and get hold of a pair of slalom poles. The front skier should have his skis pointing straight down the fall line and should be holding on to one end of the poles. The second skier should then grasp the other end of the poles from behind. (If you cannot find any slalom poles, then attach two pairs of ski poles together by looping the straps of one pair over the baskets of the other.) The second skier acts as a brake for the one in front by making short-radius turns, while the one in front skis straight down the fall line. Try this exercise on a flat slope until you feel comfortable with it before moving to more difficult slopes. You will find this exercise to be a real challenge. Keep at it – it is well worth the effort.

How it feels and where it feels

The skier in front will feel a strong braking effect when his partner turns out of the fall line, then a release as his partner comes into the fall line again.

The skier behind will feel his upper body being pulled downhill as he turns out of the fall line. This pull puts you into a very good angulated position, so you can get that extra little bit of edge needed for a good edge set. As the skier behind approaches the fall line, his skis will accelerate. Most of the time he will find himself well balanced as his arms must be out in front of his body to hold on to the poles.

The pole plant

The pole plant is probably the root of most skiing faults. Ski poles are used as a turning aid, a balancing aid and for support during the initiation phase of a turn. They are always planted towards the inside of the turn you intend to make. In the early stages, ski poles usually complicate swinging, but later they are a great help. Planting your pole is like everything else in skiing: how and when you use it will depend on the particular situation in which you find yourself. If you watch the world-class racers you will probably discover that, at times, they do not plant their poles at all.

The way you plant your ski poles helps characterize your personal skiing style. How you plant them depends on where you are holding your arms and how long your poles are. The correct length of ski pole is easily determined (see Chapter 1). Even so, you still see people skiing with the wrong length of pole. This causes a multitude of other problems, like bending at the waist if the poles are too short or throwing the arms upwards to prevent the poles from hitting the snow if they are too long.

There is an area in front of the body (never behind) where the arms should move. One of the golden rules in ski racing is 'arms in front'. To help you find that area, borrow a friend's ski pole and put it under both arms across the chest and make a few runs.

When you come to plant your pole, stop and think for a second. Where does your pole plant fit into the turn? It is definitely part of the turn. It comes at the end of one turn and at the beginning of another. Better still,

The pole should not be planted by throwing the arm forwards (above left). Instead, you should use your wrist and elbow to plant the pole somewhere between the ski tips and binding (above), depending on the steepness of the terrain

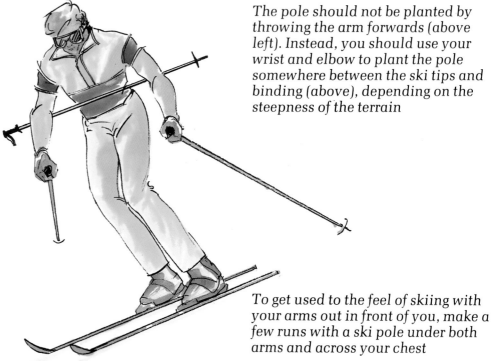

To get used to the feel of skiing with your arms out in front of you, make a few runs with a ski pole under both arms and across your chest

instead of centred over the middle of your skis. As a remedy, try concentrating on your pole planting on easier terrain. Talking out loud to give yourself verbal cues such as 'pole out' might also help.

Holding on to your pole plant too long (far left) will put you off balance in the fall line. Practise your pole plant on easier terrain (left) so that you can concentrate fully on this aspect of your skiing

think of the end of your previous turn as being the beginning of your following turn. That is where the pole plant fits in. In up unweighted turns, this is the instant when you reach the down of the down phase.

Where you plant your pole depends upon the speed at which you are travelling, the radius of your last turn and the radius of your next turn, the steepness of the slope and the effectiveness of your edge set. However, do not let all this complicate and confuse you. A good rule of thumb is to plant your pole between the ski tips and binding. In longer turns, it should be more towards the tip. In shorter turns it should be more towards the binding and a little out to the side. On steep slopes, plant your pole more downhill.

The pole should be planted by using the wrist and elbow, not by throwing the whole arm and shoulder forwards. This gesture is totally meaningless and causes the torso to swing forwards which in turn puts you off balance. It also accounts for the washing-out of the downhill ski and in extreme cases falling into the hill. Practise the pole plant on terrain that you can master easily. This allows you to concentrate fully on the pole plant.

Once you have planted your pole, it is a signal that you should be starting a new turn. As soon as you are on your way into a new turn, the pole should be removed immediately and your arm brought forwards. If you hold on to your pole plant too long, you will get thrown off balance and your weight will be put back on your ski tails as you come into the fall line

How it feels and where it feels
Your ski pole is not some kind of tree that you plant into the ground. The word 'plant' always gives the impression that it should be pushed into the snow as far as it will go. On the contrary, sometimes the pole is only touched and not planted with brute strength. Of course, it depends on the terrain and speed, as well as the kind of turns you are making. In slalom, ski racers rely greatly on their poles, using them very aggressively. However, as a general rule try a touch instead of a deliberate jab.

Skiing with your feet too close together

It is extremely encouraging to see that more and more skiers have realized that, in order to ski well, you do not have to glue your feet together. However, many skiers still think that if they get their feet close together they are skiing well. The very fact that they are trying to keep them together prohibits any further improvement. Some skiers have paid a fortune to skiing instructors just to learn how to keep their feet together and ski as if they have one leg instead of two.

If you find you are skiing with your feet too close together, and that it is prohibiting your progress and you would like to do something about it, read on!

Skiers are beginning to realize that functional skiing is a more efficient and natural way to ski. This is one of the reasons why all racers build an X-position or an A-frame at the end of their turns.

The A-frame has many advantages, one being that you can edge the downhill ski much more without losing your balance. Far too often, skiers lose their balance simply because their stance is too closed. To achieve maximum edge grip, the knee must be moved laterally as well as forwards. With an open stance you can get much more lateral movement in the knees without losing your balance. Another advantage of the A-frame is that it helps you get on to your new downhill ski much earlier in a more balanced position. A further advantage is that the upper body is always in a neutral position which allows freedom of movement, an essential element in good skiing. Also, it is a much more relaxed and

fun way to ski.

Below are a few ways to get out of the 'feet-glued-together' habit and into a new world of relaxed and skilful skiing:

1 Spread your skis to start the turn. At first, start off by spreading them as far apart as you can, then adjust them until you can get them hip-width apart. This will definitely increase independent leg action, which is needed for high-quality steering.
2 In the steering phase of the turn, lay your downhill knee against your uphill calf. This is impossible if your skis are together. By doing this, you will notice improvement in your edging ability.
3 While you are skiing, keep checking the distance between your feet. Experiment with everything from an extremely wide stance to a very narrow one. Then find what is most

To ski in a relaxed, natural way (above), you must avoid the 'feet-glued-together' habit (above left)

comfortable for you, and try to incorporate it into your everyday skiing. Hip-width is usually the most functional and comfortable width.

How it feels and where it feels
If your progress is being hindered because your skis are too close together, you will feel as if you are continually off balance and turns will be very hard to initiate. If you adopt a wider stance, it will give you a more secure, balanced feeling. Turns will also be easier to initiate. In the steering phase of the turn you will feel pressure along the inside arch of the downhill foot, around the ankle area and at the top of the inside boot shaft.

On sitting back

This problem was more apparent in the late 1960s and early 1970s. The reason for it was the appearance of the new high-back boots, the rear spoilers of which skiers were using as leaning posts. Some teaching systems even tried to capitalize on this trend. There were extreme turns at all levels, even snowplough jets.

Today, however, sitting back still poses a problem because it puts you in a very unbalanced position on skis, undermining the benefits of good posture. Generally speaking, if you are sitting back you cannot cope with changes in the terrain, and the blocked position you adopt makes it hard for you to control your skis. Racers do get back on the tails of their skis, but only when the situation allows it, usually towards the end of a turn. This tail weighting has many advantages for them, but they nearly always manage to get back into a ready position over their skis for the next turn.

A good way to overcome this problem of sitting back is to try to ski a few runs with the top two buckles of your boots undone. This will definitely make you stay in the middle of your skis. If you find that too difficult, then simply loosen the boots as much as possible and make a few runs.

Sitting back on your skis (above) makes it difficult for you to control them. You need to stay in a ready position over your skis (above right) so that you can cope with changes in terrain

How it feels and where it feels

If you are sitting back against the boot spoilers, you might get the impression that it is easier to initiate the turn. This is because your skis are flat. If you ski fast you will almost certainly have the feeling that you are a little out of control. When you are standing on the correct spot, you will know almost as if by instinct.

Leaning away from obstacles

Most skiers react to obstacles in the same way. That is, they lean away from them to avoid them, which is the most natural thing to do. In doing so, however, they forget about their skis. A typical example is when one skier tries to avoid colliding with another. The first skier usually manages to miss the second skier with his body but not with his skis or lower legs.

Instead of moving your body out of the way, try standing correctly on your skis and concentrate on directing your skis past the obstacle. Your body will automatically follow.

Chapter 5 SKIING IN DIFFICULT CONDITIONS

Skiing is fundamentally an activity that allows you to travel over snow with the minimum of effort. Your ability to do this, however, can be affected, even upset, by the ever-changing condition of the snow and whether it is on level or sloping ground. Being able to recognize these variations and cope with them with skill and ease should be the aim of the experienced skier wanting to become truly proficient. If you move away from official runs to discover the exhilaration of off-piste skiing beware of the potential dangers. Learn to respond to the special physical and technical demands of skiing in difficult conditions and enjoy your skiing experience to the full.

Reading the terrain

It has been said that snow is one of the most changeable substances known to man. The true all-round skier, therefore, is the one who can move off piste into untracked snow, deep snow, crusty snow, slush and ice and cope with all these variations with ease.

How can you, as a good parallel piste skier, extend your skiing repertoire in this way? The essential element is to have sound basic technique, technique that can be applied with the minimum of effort and preferably by habit. For once the going gets tough there will be too many other demands on your attention. You will be attempting to recognize and come to terms with the snow type and terrain, both of which may be rapidly changing. The difficult conditions you are likely to encounter include the following, either individually or in combination:

1 Deep new cold snow (perfect powder)
2 Deep new warm snow (crud)
3 Untracked snow with a crust
4 Moguls (bumps)
5 Steep snow
6 Ice
7 Fresh snow through trees
8 Narrow tracks
9 Frozen ruts
10 Slush (end of season)
11 Windblown snow ('dead snow')
12 Flat light

As in any activity that involves a degree of risk, it goes without saying that your equipment must be in good order and appropriate to the task. You must also realize that until you become at ease with the difficult conditions in which you find yourself, your body is going to be working that little bit harder and you should, therefore, be as fit and warm as possible.

When skiing on good pistes you need to pay attention to standing comfortably on your skis so that the appropriate technique can be applied with ease (good posture). You also need to look at the ground ahead, not only to choose a path but also to assess the type of snow and how much pressure and edge need to be applied to the skis in order to make them grip the ground. This assessment of the snow is one of the keys to skiing in difficult conditions. Skiing is fundamentally the passage of the skis either over or through the snow and, depending on the consistency of the snow, the skis need various degrees of input in terms of turning, pressure and edging.

Michael Mair of Italy uses all his skill to tackle the icy downhill course at Kitzbühel, Austria

Snow is affected by wind and temperature. The former can transport snow from one site to another and, in so doing, can cause damage to the crystals. The tiny arms of the crystals are broken off the control body which results in the ice particles being more compact either once the wind has dropped or a lee slope has been found. Snow transported and damaged in this way is called 'dead snow' or 'windblown snow' and can be recognized by its dullness, lack of sparkle and inability to fluff up when disturbed by a passing ski.

Temperature also has an effect on the snow cover. Low temperatures preserve the snow allowing little or no change in its state, while a rise in temperature allows the snow cover to settle, compact and even disappear through evaporation. Combinations of wind and temperature can produce a crust on the snow surface which can vary both in thickness and strength. Sometimes this crust is sufficiently strong to support a skier and at other times it is not. It is not uncommon to find both supportive and unsupportive crust on a single run.

If you have developed sound, effective and efficient techniques for skiing on piste, not a great deal has to change in order to cope with more demanding situations. In fact, the major change needs to be a mental one; an appreciation of how differently the various types of snow and terrain affect the skis.

Coping with powder snow

Skiing in deep powder snow is the type of skiing that a great many skiers aspire to. Indeed, beautiful action photographs showing people 'skiing powder' are very often used to sell ski holidays and equipment. So, what is powder snow and how do you cope with it?

Genuine powder snow exists when the degree of moisture in the air and the temperature are such that complete snow crystals are formed. That is, crystals of the shape you see in Christmas decorations. These crystals/snowflakes arrive without any wind that may damage them and settle slowly. Because they all land intact and are not compressed by subsequent flakes, a large amount of air is trapped within the snow layer and the snow has a sparkling effect. An area of powder snow will, when hit with a ski pole, billow up into a cloud and settle down again slowly.

Because of the amount of air within the snow layer and the fact that the majority of the snowflakes have not stuck together, there is very little resistance offered by the snow cover when a skier skis through it. And because of this lack of resistance even thigh-deep powder is relatively easy to ski through. However, the difficulties lie in not being able to see your skis all the time and the uncertainty of what lies beneath the snow surface. The latter consideration is very important early in the season when snow depth may not be great and tree trunks and fallen branches can be close to the surface.

Popular films and videos have suggested that when skiing deep powder snow you should sit back and

The epitome of deep powder skiing

move as slowly as the slow-motion pictures indicate. Nothing could be further from the truth. To sit back would mean a change in basic posture and increased difficulty in applying technique. Remember that your legs can only work well provided that you stand above your feet. To sit or lean back would mean putting your leg muscles into a supportive rather than an active state, thereby reducing their ability to turn.

Although true powder snow offers little resistance, there is of course some. This is created by your legs passing through the snow and will depend on the depth of the snow. In order to overcome this added resistance you have two choices. One is to look for and ski down steeper slopes. The steepness will give you the extra speed required to bash through the snow cover. The second is to decrease the frequency of your turning so that what turns you make are done at a higher speed.

The turning technique in powder can either be conventional up un-weighting parallel turns or compression turns. With the up un-weighting technique it is important to make the up movement strong without being jerky, and some hip rotation can aid the initiation of the turn. Of course this is the only situation where hip rotation can be considered useful. At other times, and especially on hard pistes, it is a positive disadvantage.

Other essential elements of technique when skiing powder are strong smooth movements, continuous turning and keeping close to the fall line. You may find it advantageous to begin a run using up motion with a little hip rotation and then, once you have established a rhythm and felt the consistency of the snow, slowly change to compression turn-type leg movements (see page 85).

Keeping the legs and feet close together and imagining that the skis are a surfboard is also a great aid. Should the slope become steeper, do not panic: maintain your rhythm, keep turning and appreciate that your lower legs are acting as a brake in the snow. Feel a wave of snow building up against your shins and slowing you down.

With good powder snow you should feel a certain amount of springiness in the snow which will help you initiate the turns and this, together with your rhythm, will give you a floating sensation. Skiing deep snow is the closest thing to flying.

In deep snow, you should bring the tips of your skis to the surface (far left) to prevent the skis from diving. The deeper the snow, the more the ski tends to fall through the snow layers. Your position over your skis should be the same as when you ski downhill parallel to the slope (left)

When skiing off piste and maybe out of sight of the main skiing thoroughfare, and out of sight of the ski patrol controlled areas, it is unwise to go it alone. Off-piste skiing is adventurous and not without its dangers. Always ski in a group, ideally never less than three; in this way, if anyone is injured one member of the party can go for help while the other stays with the victim.

Remember, too, that the group's safety can be jeopardized should any skier lose a ski. You should, therefore, wear powder leashes so that valuable time in finding rejected skis is not lost. If the snow is really deep, over the knee, you will find it essential to wear goggles. Powder snow is so light that its disturbance by your skis will send it billowing up into your face as you ski. It goes without saying that a neck scarf, high collar or roll-neck shirts are a must as powder snow will take great delight in finding warm

flesh on which to settle.

When out with friends there always tends to be a race to descend through untracked snow. In fact, a great deal can be learned about the condition of the snow by watching others tackle it.

As the first skier goes down take note of whether the snow billows up in a cloud of dust or a cloud of chunks. Dust cloud means soft powder with little resistance. Chunks indicate consolidated snow. Once the leading skier has made a few turns take a close look at his tracks. How deep are they? Has he turned his skis in the snow or brought them to the surface? Are the edges of the tracks well-defined and sharp, has the snow run back into them leaving a soft, round edge? Making careful notes like this will help prepare you for the run ahead. These clues will help you decide where to go and how much effort to put into those all-important first few turns.

Windblown snow

Windblown snow is snow that has been transported from one part of the mountain to another by the wind. During its transportation the tiny arms of each crystal have been broken off and when finally it settles each ice particle which is at the centre of each snowflake comes closer together than is possible in powder snow.

Consequently, the snow cover has less air within it and tends to settle and consolidate more quickly. Because of this the snow cover presents a great deal more resistance to any passing ski and does not billow up into a cloud of dust but instead breaks into chunks. It can also be recognized by its dull, flat texture. This type of snow can be found in hollows and lee slopes. If found in small quantities in hollows it is best to negotiate it by running straight through it and turning on or in more sympathetic snow on the far side. On lee slopes where large areas can be found, it needs to be approached with aggression, power and some speed. But beware, lee slopes are notorious places for avalanche danger.

You will find a reluctance by the ski to travel sideways within the snow and an exaggerated inward lean of the legs is a must in order to be successful. Speed and courage are also essential.

If the snow proves to be deeper than knee height, it may be better to lift the total ski length out of the snow to turn them. On steeper ground this type of snow is prone to avalanche so, once again, beware. Falls in this type of snow can cause twisting injuries as the snow traps the ski while the body, arms and legs continue to fall and twist. Make sure you check your bindings and treat this snow type with caution.

When skiing through large areas of windblown snow, you need to approach it with aggression, power and speed

Mogul skiing

As you ski over the top of each bump, use the lack of resistance between ski and snow to turn your skis

Wherever a ski trail becomes a little steeper, skiers tend to turn more often and, in so doing, wear away the snow cover. As more skiers use similar turning points the repeated passage of skiers accentuates this wear and eventually large bumps or mounds – moguls – begin to appear between the ski tracks. On softish snow, moguls of a few feet high can be created within half an hour and continue to grow until the track is worn down to ground level.

Ski control can be maintained provided that the skis are in contact with the ground. Just as a car that becomes airborne after driving over a humpback bridge cannot be accelerated, slowed down or turned until the wheels are back on the ground, neither can a ski. Bumpy ground tends to throw a skier into the air and the all-essential ski-ground contact is lost, giving rise to great discomfort and maybe even loss of balance. Essentially, the technique required to overcome this is one that keeps the skis on the ground.

Compression turns provide the key. Instead of standing high on each bump, the skier allows his legs to bend. In fact, he lets the ground push his feet up towards his torso without distorting the upper body in any way. The feeling is of bringing the knees up in front of you, a feeling that your heel bindings are about to hit you in the buttocks. Once over the bump the knack is to extend your legs again with some force into the hollow and thus press the skis hard into the ground. (See also Chapter 2, Schussing over bumps.)

Once you have mastered straight runs over successive bumps without

Mogul skiing

becoming airborne, you need to become aware that as the skis pass over the summit of each bump there is a moment when a large part of them is off the ground. They are thus easy to turn because of the lack of resistance. If you combine this bending of the legs with their turning on the summit of each bump followed by the extension of the legs into the hollows you will soon be able to negotiate a series of bumps without becoming airborne and losing control. The more proficient you become at this, the greater the speed at which you can travel.

However, there will be times when even competent bending, turning and stretching will not keep you on the ground. As your speed increases, begin to ski through the hollows – they have 'passes' or 'cols' within them where it is possible to turn the skis. As you ski the hollows you will require far less bending and extending of the legs and you will be able, therefore, to travel faster.

Choosing which way to go has always been an initial problem in mogul skiing. There are two ways of visualizing a path. The first is to treat the bumps as slalom poles and ski around them; or, second, imagine yourself standing at the top of a series of bumps with a bucket full of dye. Pour the dye on to the ground and watch it flow down the slope and around the bumps. It takes the easiest path. This is the path that your feet should follow. To help you achieve this, it is important to ski down close to the fall line and use lots of anticipation. Begin your bump skiing career on gentle ground, gradually building up the distance between stops. Although you may admire the ease with which good bump skiers seem to perform, you must realize that they are in fact working very hard and never being complacent.

As you become more at ease and comfortable on bumpy terrain, study other skiers as they ski through the undulations. Take note of where they place their feet and consequently their skis. Try to imagine the best possible way of getting your skis to grip the snow. There are of course areas of snow within a mogul field that mechanically help the ski to bite and hold the ground and others that offer no help whatsoever. When the going gets tough, always imagine the task that your skis have to do and then try to choose a path that will give them the best possible advantage.

A word of warning – skiing the bumps is very much a gymnastic activity. Never do it first thing in the morning without thoroughly warming up first. It tests and loads the body joints, with the back and knees coming top of the list. Talking of good bump skiing in the hotel is a lot easier and safer than the real thing the next morning!

Frozen ruts

Slalom courses inevitably become full of ruts, making it difficult to ski smoothly

Late in the season, when the days become longer and warmer, the snow invariably becomes soft and wet. The tracks left behind by skiers become deeper and the lumps of disturbed snow tend to remain prominent. All this damage to the snow cover is then frozen solid as night falls, and the following morning, unless the piste machines have been out, the skiing surface is full of ruts.

Each rut can either trap a ski or the small snow walls can act as kerbs that catch out any ski that hits them broadside. To ski smoothly over such a surface is impossible. The very fact that the skis need to be lifted over the frozen ruts to turn dictates that in order to be safe you must do a great deal of hopping or jumping to turn.

While travelling between turns the frozen surface will try its hardest to deflect the passage of your skis and will offer a very bumpy ride. All you can do is to be sure that the skis receive sufficient pressure to keep them on course and to maintain good posture by holding a flexible body that is able to absorb all the jolts. Any turns need to be done on the smoothest areas that can be found, and need to be of the jump variety, in order to prevent a turning ski hitting a small ice wall. Aim to take off strongly and land lightly and steer very positively to ensure a safe passage.

Skiing through the hollows of a mogul field (left) will enable you to travel faster since it requires less bending and extending of the legs

Flat light and white-out conditions

It is not until you are blindfolded for a short time and asked to perform a few easy and familiar tasks that you come to realize how much we all take sight for granted. Static activities such as combing your hair or cleaning your teeth become major challenges. As soon as you need to move, the problems seem to become insurmountable. Vision is essential to mobile activity and performance drops drastically as the quality of vision fades.

When skiing, the eyes are liable to a multitude of abuses. It can be very cold and the eyes can water; it can be hot and sweat can drip into them. When the sun comes out, the glare can be damaging, and when the light fades your eyes have to strain to distinguish between uphill and downhill as your perception of where the horizon is becomes unclear. The ability to ski well in 'flat light' is something all newcomers to the sport long for and all experts secretly wish they could do better. It is something that comes with familiarity and confidence. Remember, those skiers who whiz past you in the mist are quite likely to be locals who know their mountainside extremely well.

Flat light will rob you of shadow and horizon. As soon as you lose these two valuable points of reference it becomes difficult to distinguish between uphill and downhill, and changes in gradient. You need to fall back on 'feeling' the ground through your feet and looking for small clues which may aid you in assessing the lie of the land. To help in this, a good pair of goggles is a must, or, if it is not snowing, a pair of quality sunglasses.

The filter effect of the lenses may just heighten sufficiently any shadows present to give you a slight advantage. Again it helps a great deal if you can ski behind someone else. How they cope can give vital clues as to the lie of the ground ahead. You can examine their ski tracks at close quarters and thereby gain some indication of steepness and consistency of snow. Skiing in flat light is always a precarious activity. Even small features in the ground, when you come across them unexpectedly, can undermine your balance. Those of major proportions may totally destroy your good posture.

In technical terms, how can you cope with it? You can only feel the ground provided that there is some pressure between your skis and the snow. Any features on the ground that tend to throw you up in the air will destroy your 'feel' for the ground and this will cause you to lose both control and stability.

As the light fails, train yourself to settle down a little more on to your skis. That is, adopt a slightly lower position. Doing this will mean that your legs are bent a little more. Should you hit that unexpected bump then there is a greater chance that the shock will be absorbed more by the legs, with less distortion and loss of balance by the upper body, rather than the whole body and legs being projected into the air.

Low cloud in Crans-Montana. Successful skiing in bad light only comes with experience

The danger of skiing in flat light is that it robs you of two valuable points of reference – shadow and horizon

A lower body position also means that by moving the knees laterally you can quickly move from one set of edges to another, and thereby from turn to turn. By turning this way and eliminating any up-down movement it is possible to maintain contact with the ground and to continue feeling the snow. In terms of feeling with your feet, this lowered body position should allow you to feel as if all the side of the outside foot while turning is against the floor of the boot and, should the ski meet any resistance to forward motion, it will lessen the chance of the upper body being thrown forwards.

If the truth were known, no one enjoys skiing in bad light and in reality it is only lots of practice in such conditions that lessens the potential fear. The absorption of knowledge can be accelerated by reading and training but there is no easy way to gain experience. That only comes with time. So to help yourself to ski better in poor light, consider these essential points and follow the advice:

1 Make sure you are as fit and healthy as possible.
2 Always wear warm clothing.
3 Take with you good goggles or sunglasses.
4 Adopt a lower body position.
5 Keep your posture low to cope with unexpected bumps.
6 Keep your feet on the ground.
7 Keep turning to maintain pressure and feel.
8 Keep your ears open – the sound of other skiers and their skis can give you vital clues.

Ice skiing

To many holiday skiers ice is loathsome. It is something they find hard to make their skis grip on to, and the noise of skis skidding over ice is something they find frightening.

It is possible to ski over ice provided that you understand the needs of your skis. For it is the skis that have to grip the ground in order to make you feel secure. Ice on mountainsides comes in several forms and experience will tell you when it is likely to occur.

Irrespective of performance level, the fundamental need of all skiers is the same: a secure base, whatever the consistency of the snow. For the ski to be able to grip very hard on snow or ice, the edges need to be sharp and flush with the running surface. Early attempts to ski on ice should be restricted to traversing across smaller patches, turning on the snow on the far side and traversing back again over the ice. When trying this, your aim should be to cut your way across the patch of ice without any loss of grip and thus without any sideways movement. This can be achieved by maintaining pressure against the working edge (inside downhill ski), remaining calm and feeling as if you are pressing against the instep of your downhill foot. Do not apply any rotational force to your leg and ski, for if you do, and the ski is turned only a few degrees, it will lose that all-important grip and your security will be sacrificed.

To ski on ice and enjoy any degree of security, two areas need to be looked at. The first is the condition of the ski edges. Without sharp edges the battle is already lost. It is worth-

while learning to sharpen your own edges (see Chapter 1). Not only will you have the knowledge that it has been done well, you will also have the reassurance that your preparation is as good as it can be. The second area is understanding how the skis behave on ice.

The forces upon the skis, their behaviour and control, can be likened to driving a car on ice. The fundamental need to grip the ground and maintain that grip is the same. The factors that are likely to destroy that security are excessive speed in relation to the amount of grip available, quick over-steering that can break the adhesion, and sudden movements that either over- or under-pressure the skis.

To negotiate ice, therefore, you must remain calm but positive. All movements need to be as smooth as possible allowing gradual increases and decreases of pressure against the skis and any rapid turning of the skis must be avoided. It is this turning or rather not turning the skis that is the key to successful ice skiing. The skis ideally need to maintain their grip on the ice for the duration of the turn. This can only be done provided that the turning skis are pressurized and edged before any turn takes place. It is only the calm application of these factors in that order that allows the preservation of the grip throughout the turn.

Filing ski edges to keep them sharp

Any sudden turning of the skis will destroy this adhesion. Consider driving a car on ice – should you suddenly turn the steering wheel, a front-wheel skid will occur. However, if you turn it gently it is possible to maintain adhesion with the front wheels and eliminate any skidding by not creating it in the first place. This is exactly what you have to achieve with your skis on ice.

The repeated passage of skiers can and does scrape areas of ice into a hard, glass-like surface, but even on such areas it is sometimes possible to detect small areas of roughness that can offer the skis some additional grip. Be sure to take advantage of those patches and turn on them.

Having initiated the turn not only does the pressure need to be maintained against the turning ski by pressing against the instep of the foot, but the degree of edge must also be kept by maintaining the correct amount of increased lean to the outside leg. Each time you turn, try to imagine that you are turning around a slalom pole and trying to brush the pole with your inside hip. All this has to be done as calmly as possible of course, even though you may be feeling great apprehension.

Success will only come with practice, but as you practise always try to imagine and feel what the needs of the skis are in a given situation and strive to meet them.

Skiing on any frozen surface requires a calm but positive approach, and good posture is essential. Take advantage of any areas of roughness in the surface to turn your skis

Understanding how you ski, and how you learn to ski, are fundamental to improving performance. Balance and co-ordination are affected by external forces beyond your control; the greater your awareness of these forces and how they work, the better your chances of skiing well. You should try not to allow irrational feelings of fear to interfere with your skiing — learn how to think positively and overcome those mental barriers. This chapter also explains the advantages of being a woman skier and how your diet and correct preparation can be invaluable aids to good skiing.

You and the mountain

In both Nordic and Alpine skiing the equipment has developed in response to the demands of the activity. Dealing with gravity or the lack of it, the use of modern materials and the demands of greater efficiency by racers have all played a part in the sport's evolution. The greatest difference between Nordic and Alpine is at the point of contact between the skier and ski. The lightweight shoes and bindings with heel lift of the Nordic skier allow for cross-country man-powered movement, while the heel-fixed bindings and laterally stiff boots assist the Alpine skier to deal with the forces generated by gravity-powered downhill skis.

Understanding Alpine skiing has been the goal of many experts over the years. Great confusion and controversy has dominated international discussion, with national ski schools tending to advocate diametrically opposed styles. Skiers going from one national ski school system to another were often confronted with having to relearn technique. However, some national ski schools and coaching schemes now recognize the common denominators of functional movement patterns. But sadly there is still no official international agreement. Since, in a quarter of a century, the question of *what* to teach has not yet been resolved it is unlikely that agreement will be reached on *how* people learn for some time.

Meanwhile, the most efficient

A mountain often appears beautiful and inviting, but its façade may be deceptive. Ultimately, your relationship with it must be guided by experience

skiers in the world – the top racers of all nationalities – demonstrate similarities rather than differences in effective body movements. The only obvious discrepancies arise from differences in structural shape, physical fitness, lengths and strengths of levers, perceptual abilities, co-ordination, personality and equipment.

Each skier is unique. The skiers' common ground is the mountain and the forces that affect them equally. Ultimately, it is the mountain that is the teacher and your relationship with it that counts. Going with the flow of gravity one moment and resisting its pull the next is the sport of skiing. Experimenting with these forces is the art of self-expression on skis.

Keeping alive at sub-zero temperatures or, more mundanely, avoiding sore feet by not having wrinkled socks, is all part of surviving in the mountains. The mountain, like the sea, has its own rules. The speed of some teaching methods, the sophistication of modern equipment and well-signposted pistes, can all lead you into a potentially dangerous world. Years of experience are ultimately your best teacher and respecting this fact is the beginning of understanding how to harmonize with the mountain.

Chapter 3 explains how a ski works. Understanding what your equipment can do for you will help you to trust the ski to respond to your actions. Many skiers imagine that skiing is basically standing on two planks which have to be heaved about, wasting untold energy in lifting and throwing their body around. When

a ski is running flat on the snow it glides in a straight line and when edged and pressured it is designed to turn in a curved arc. Realizing that skis are gliding *and* turning machines may alter the way you both ride and guide them.

Erika Hess of Switzerland, one of the best all-round women skiers on the circuit. Like all racers, she trusts her skis to respond to her actions and the demands of the terrain

Dynamic balance

Skiing is essentially all about dealing with the unexpected. The game is to balance, to flow with gravity and use muscles to change body shape, resisting the external forces generated by this movement over a slippery, tilted surface. Once in motion you must respond to the demands of *dynamic* rather than *static* balance.

Orientation in this radically different world requires body awareness, active vision, alert hearing, and good dynamic balance. Rather like the tennis player about to receive a serve, you need to adopt a posture or body shape that is ready for instant action, prepared for ever-changing terrain and snow conditions (see also Chapter 2).

Dynamic balance differs from static balance in several ways. We generally stand on our heels, arms by our sides with our body mass directly above the feet. When coping with the dynamics of motion:

1 The body mass lowers through flexing hips, knees and ankles.
2 The weight moves forwards and is felt over the whole foot with the instep and ball of the foot most actively used in skiing.
3 In turning, the centre of mass does not stay over the feet, but inclines inwards.
4 The pelvis tilts upwards so that the legs can become active.
5 The arms move forwards and outwards, hanging freely from the shoulders, and ready to assist in balancing.
6 The head needs to be kept still with the eyes level and actively reading the terrain.

To remain in dynamic balance you should be aware of the forces at work as you turn. Centripetal force, which makes your skis turn around a central point due to their design, and snow resistance are the external forces acting on you when you turn

The effects of gravity

In attempting an understanding of skiing, Sir Isaac Newton provides us with some relatively simple explanations of bodies in motion. Understanding the mechanics of skiing may not change your ability to control a pair of skis, but when face down in the snow understanding that a movable force has just met an immovable object might be of some solace.

Newton's First Law states that a body remains at rest or in uniform motion in a straight line unless acted upon by a force. So to get your mass in motion you need muscles or gravity to counteract 'inertia'. Once in motion down a slope and under the effect of gravity and inertia (momentum) you have to create a force in order to alter your direction or speed. In skiing it is not always desirable to go down every slope in a straight line. By changing direction and lengthening your route you can avoid obstacles and control your speed.

The forces that you need to make a turn are snow resistance and centripetal force. Turning, edging and applying pressure to the ski sets up these forces and the result is a turning arc. This arc usually involves some lateral drift or skidding which are a result of your momentum carrying you on in the original direction.

The important thing here is the resulting change of shape both to the snow and to your body. The snow is pushed to the side while your body compensates for the pull of momentum to the outside of the turn by maintaining the centre of mass inside the turning arc. You will feel the pressure of these combined forces through your feet.

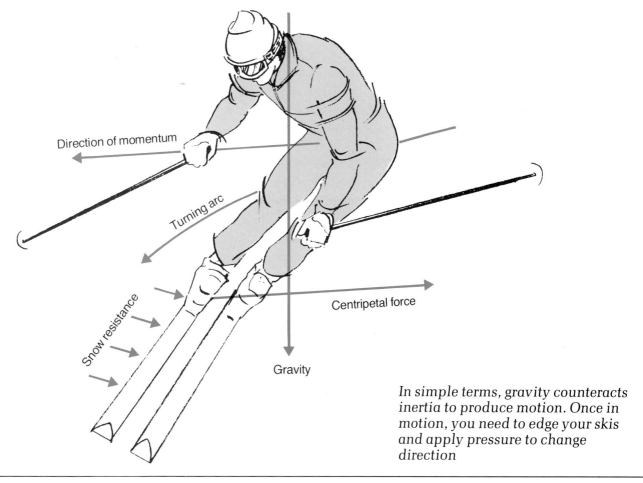

Direction of momentum

Turning arc

Snow resistance

Centripetal force

Gravity

In simple terms, gravity counteracts inertia to produce motion. Once in motion, you need to edge your skis and apply pressure to change direction

The effects of gravity

In order not to topple over by banking the whole body inwards, the upper body is flexed forwards at the hips and remains facing the direction of momentum while the thighs rotate in the pelvis directing the path of the turn. This gives rise to the curved shape of a skier, called angulation (see Chapter 3), which is sometimes misinterpreted as a sideways bending of the waist.

Newton's Third Law states that any force on a body produces an equal and opposite reaction. This has many implications for you as a skier. Any unnecessary movement of your arms or upper body requires an opposite reaction to compensate and vice versa. On the other hand, powerful movements of the legs can be counter-balanced with a movement of the upper body. When you lose balance, an appropriate 're-action' of the arms can re-establish your equilibrium. Observe yourself running, as one leg moves forwards the opposite arm compensates for the disturbance.

The complexity of organizing the controlled, balanced movement of a central body mass with a jointed collection of levers over a continually changing mountainside is a task that defeats our intellect, which operates in a linear, verbal, logical fashion.

Thousands of chemical and electrical impulses are computed simultaneously by the central nervous system. Anticipating the combined forces of gravity and momentum through our senses and responding appropriately is a highly complex operation. We can read all the books and theorize *ad infinitum* but how do you get your body to understand?

Skiing is a dance with the mountain and you must flow with this partner. Only the dancer, the moving body, can fully appreciate the subtlety of the blending that makes you one in a non-verbal world of movement and feeling.

Flowing with the mountain is the end product of a complex interaction between the physical world and your body. It is essential to anticipate and control the combined forces of gravity and momentum

Do you know how to learn?

Contrary to popular belief a teacher cannot make learning happen. A teacher can only create an environment within which you can safely explore your limits, adapt what you already know; encouraging and guiding you to stretch into new experiences. The learning happens *inside you* so you must take ultimate responsibility for it.

Your body already knows a lot about balance. Every day it gets you up and organizes your standing, walking, running and maintains all the plumbing, heating, sewage and energy systems. If you treat it well it will give you good service. Trust it to learn to ski too!

Recent research into different brain functions has changed our understanding of human learning and performance. Like a heat-seeking missile we are programmed to reach realistic predetermined goals given adequate accurate feedback in relation to the goal. In simple terms, we are learners. You may have forgotten how, but your capacity to learn only needs to be rediscovered. Given that the goal is clear and achievable your body will take care of the 'how' as long as you trust and stay absorbed in the whole process.

Learning habits

You will need to develop habits that support the process of learning, recognizing that rates of progress fluctuate and that practice with awareness makes perfect:

1 Things may get worse before they get better. As an old pattern or 'habit' is regrooved into a new movement it may feel very awkward. As muscle

memory increases and learning takes place these feelings will disappear so that the new becomes familiar and comfortable.

2 Severe judgments inhibit learning. Be patient and allow your body to make the necessary corrections.

3 Trying too hard wastes energy, creates unnecessary tension and interferes with muscle movement.

4 Expectations pitched too high interfere with enjoyment, learning and performance. Comparing what you think *should be* with what *is* only creates disappointment. On the other hand, expectations pitched too low tend to be self-fulfilling prophecies. Are your expectations of the weather or speed of progress realistic? If they are not, can you let go of them and accept what *is* happening?

5 Balance your learning. Mix the periods of focused concentration on your movements with more playful, broadly-focused attention so that you do not get stale. Also, mix periods of

Ski school creates an environment in which you can explore your limits

skiing within your 'comfort' zone with some 'stretch' and vice versa if you tend always to ski at your limit.

6 Avoid extreme stress. The two extremes on the spectrum from boredom to panic are not useful states in which to learn something new or perform what you have already learned. If you find yourself on boring terrain, take advantage of it to explore the subtleties of your movements and improve your balance. If you find yourself out of your depth, take the lift down; it is easier than walking.

7 Enjoy yourself. Keep an eye on your fun meter. Enjoyment and learning seem to go hand in hand. If you are frustrated or upset look for the cause; is it inappropriate terrain, unprepared or inappropriate equipment, lack of concentration, trying too hard, fear or fatigue?

Body and mind in harmony

You need your intellect and reasoning abilities to select the resort, choose which slope to ski down and decide on what you are going to focus your attention. However, once your body is in motion, the commentator, the verbal part, needs to take a back seat. Unfortunately, since it likes to be in control, it may not want to be a passenger. By involving it in the pathfinding and observing role of co-pilot and radio ham you can create harmony between body and mind. This co-operation is an essential part of performance and learning.

There are various obstacles that prevent your body from seeing, hearing, and feeling, and from being in the 'here and now'. Fear, self-doubt, and trying too hard all start with thoughts about the way you perceive your ability to cope. These thoughts of past or future set up tension and resistance which distort body shape and block sensory feedback. Thinking about skiing as you ride a lift or stand at the top of a slope needs to be a constructive rather than a destructive use of your imagination.

Getting to know yourself
The mountains offer an unparalleled opportunity to harmonize with the elements. Everyone has different reasons for learning to ski, whether for adventure, fresh air, exercise, a suntan, socializing or simply a change of scene. What are yours? Perhaps you are skiing because you enjoy the exhilaration of sliding or the challenge of meeting your fears.

It is useful to understand what motivates you to ski and to clarify the long-term direction that you would like your skiing to take. How would you like to be skiing next year or the year after? Is this dream realistic? What steps are you going to have to take to make this a reality? Write down some of the things that you would like to achieve on your next ski holiday. By becoming conscious of what you want you will be much more likely to notice any conflicting goals and lack of direction.

Knowing where you are now
Your eyes, ears, nose and other sense organs let your body know what is in the physical world and where it is in relation to you. These 'feelers' let your body have the necessary input to make the fine adjustments to keep you in balance.

Your body does not speak English or French and the more you think 'verbally' the less you can feel. Skiing is an activity that requires a different sort of brain functioning. You need to tune into body language rather than mind talk. Bodyspeak is moving pictures, whole movement patterns, spatial awareness, rhythm, symbols and images. The body needs to know where it is and to adjust to where it is going. The information is all there – it is just a question of tuning in the receivers and turning up the volume.

Whatever your aims in skiing terms, make sure they are realistic

Successful skiing requires you to be aware at all times of the physical world so that your body can make the necessary adjustments to stay in balance

Explore your senses

To quieten your mind and get involved with the action of skiing, explore what is happening by asking yourself one of the following questions as you ski:

1 What are you *seeing* and where are you looking?
2 What are you *hearing* and what are you listening for?
3 What are you *feeling*?

Choose some easy terrain and stick to one question at a time to avoid scattering your attention. Ideally all your 'feelers' need to be on the alert. As you get used to greater input you will notice how thoughts interfere and fear creates tunnel vision. You may notice that one or all of these senses are not participating as much as they could.

Conditions such as flat light and fog can cause anxiety in even the most experienced skiers. Many people actually make matters worse by saying 'I cannot see anything' and then stop looking! Slow down, get your general bearings from piste markers, noises of lifts, other skiers and then with 'soft focus' look for distinctions in the snow surface. Ski tracks and mounds of snow do show up. This is a great opportunity to heighten your awareness of hearing and feeling and help your body to balance.

Learning how to stay in the present is an art. Choosing the right terrain for your level of ability is at the crux of this. Play it safe rather than sorry and practise concentration and awareness games to hold your attention on what is happening rather than what is not. Ask yourself these questions: *where* do I feel? *when* do I feel? *how much* on a scale of one to ten? Once you can feel what, where, when and how much then you can experiment with 'what if'.

Practise exploring your senses on easy terrain so that your concentration is not distracted by anxiety or fear

When you are skiing off piste, you should always tune in your senses to what is happening around you

What to look for

The 'flow' (fall) line
Where you want to go (noticing other skiers, rocks or trees and seeing the ideal route)
Seeing the next three turns
Differences in snow texture
Snow patches rather than ice patches
The path rather than the drop off
Contours and 'line' in the moguls
Shadows on a sunny day
Your shadow on a back-lit slope

What to listen for

The sound of your skis
Differences between left and right turns
Differences in snow texture
Differences in carved or skidded turns
Your pole plant
The squeak of your boots
Your clothing as you move
Your breathing
The rush of the air past your ears
Other skiers
Mechanical sounds of piste machines or ski lifts

What to feel for

The contact of your feet on the snow
The pressure change from foot to foot
The percentage of weight on each foot
The pressure build-up in the turn
Your shins on the front of your boots
The ball of the foot, instep and heel as you turn
Degree of edge of the skis
The touch of your pole plant
The moment of edge change
The flow of your 'centre' into the turn
The 'floating' ski/little toe

Getting ready to ski

To ski well you must not be over-stressed or tense. The back of the boots, straight-legged skier is expressing fear that is either current or was experienced as a beginner. You must allow your body whatever time it needs to become comfortable, so that you can be an active and willing passenger on the skis. Start the day on easy runs to warm up and finish the day on easy runs to end on a good note, and avoid the frustration of falling from fatigue.

A warm-up and stretch before you set off are a great way of getting in touch with your body. Are you breathing sufficiently? Focus on inhaling and exhaling from your centre. Anxiety and tense breathing go hand in hand. Tune into the present by closing your eyes and observing your breathing.

Then do a body check. In particular, pay attention to any tension in your shoulders, arms and hands. Move down your body, feel your feet, where is your weight? Are your toes relaxed? Can you feel the front of your boots? Can your ankles flex freely? Open your eyes, have a good look at the slope and choose an ideal route.

Overcoming interference

Come back to observing your breathing before you set off and count to yourself one, two, three as you inhale, and one, two, three, four as you exhale. Allow yourself to stay with this exercise as you set off, noticing if your attention is distracted by any thoughts. Allow them to pass by and refocus on the breathing exercise. It is important to get to know your brand of interference and your thought patterns so that you can notice them intruding earlier and refocus sooner. They can knock at the door but you do not have to let them in.

Other ways of tuning into body-speak are to sing songs that suit the rhythm of the slope or to play imagination games. Some people like to listen to music while they ski, others find it distracting since it cuts out other useful sounds. If so, play the music on the lift to give you a rhythmical feeling and then turn it off while you ski.

Concentration is as much a part of a racer's skill as physical strength or technique. Leonard Stock of Austria (above) practises shutting out all interference

Most skiers experience fear of falling over at some time in their career. Overcoming this fear relies on you keeping it in proper perspective

Overcoming fear

If a crevasse were actually to open up in front of you and a snow snake to raise its head and hiss, you would probably experience 'real' fear. The situation would demand an instant and appropriate response for your survival. Your body's fight or flight mechanism would pump adrenaline into your system to prepare you for action. Blood sugar level, heart rate and blood pressure would all increase for expected energy demands. You would leap over the yawning void and get away from danger, amazing yourself with above-average strength. Snow snakes apart, this is how you would respond to an immediate and real danger.

The most common obstacle to progress in skiing is irrational or imagined fear, either worrying about the future or regretting the past. It might feel very real while you are caught up in it but it is usually based on illusion. Unfortunately, it often becomes a self-fulfilling prophecy. This then adds reinforcement for next time so

that you really believe it!

You may well have experienced some, or even all, of the most common fears expressed by skiers. The fear of falling over and injuring yourself is usually accompanied by that of losing control of your skis, going too fast and not being able to stop. For beginners in particular there is often nervousness about what others might think if they fall over, and the worry of not being able to get it right. Other skiers fear success just as much as they fear failure; for them, a reputation to live up to is as undesirable as feeling unable to learn.

The downward spiral
With an imagined or irrational fear buzzing around your head you are in fact focusing on what you least want. Vision narrows, distorting reality and robbing the body of vital feedback. The body responds by tensing up and holding back, putting the skeleton off balance and wasting energy. Breathing becomes tense, preventing ade-

quate oxygen intake. The sensation of speed distorts so that it seems faster than it actually is. The pelvis tilts so that the back hollows and the legs lose their strength. The sense of insecurity grows until panic is reached.

Perhaps you do not reach the bottom of the spiral and your anxiety just produces aching thighs, or awkward, jerky movements. It is likely that trying even harder or greater resistance is your next response. Since both interfere with performance it is likely that you have attracted or created exactly what you most feared. And so it goes on . . . downhill all the way.

Real or imagined fear?
Recognizing the difference between real and imagined fear is the first step to overcoming it. Real fear would be experienced if you stood at the top of a black run when you only ever ski blue ones. This sort of fear is based on self-preservation. Listen to it telling you to take the lift down!

If the fear is not of an immediate danger the cure is to become involved in the present rather than the future or the past. As with everything, practice makes perfect! If you get used to doing a 'centring' concentration exercise when you do not really need it, you will have trust in it when you do. Start by focusing on the physical manifestations of your anxiety: tense breathing; butterflies in the stomach; gripping your ski poles too tightly; curled up toes; tight shoulders; rigid ankles and knees. Usually your body will let go of the tension once you pay attention to it. If it persists, focus more deeply on it by rating its intensity on a scale of one to ten.

Think positively

What you see is what you get! If you believe you are unco-ordinated, you will be. Your attitude and beliefs about yourself will help shape your performance. A self-image is made up of thoughts, other people's opinions, your unique past history, and will differ from role to role. It is usually inaccurate and often incomplete. Moreover, people nowadays tend to emphasize negative rather than positive results, the 'what you did wrong' rather than 'what you did right'.

You can start to revamp your self-image miles away from the ski slopes by giving it a spring-clean; throw out all the tatty baggage of past failures and redress the balance. Write down six things that you have achieved on skis and leave false modesty behind. Every time you make a negative judgment, make a note so that you begin to realize how you are guilty of sabotaging your best efforts. Notice how critical and unforgiving you are, dwelling on what did not work rather than what did.

Visualization

Visualization is now widely accepted as a valuable contribution to performance and learning. Using your imagination to recreate the sights, sounds and feelings that you experience as you ski will keep the neural pathways active since your body does not know the difference between the real experience and one that is vividly imagined. So daydreaming during the months between skiing holidays may not be as frivolous as it sounds. Regular, short practices can enhance your performance, adding to

your confidence, self-image and smoothing out your movements.

Choose a quiet place and sit with your spine supported and your arms and legs uncrossed. Close your eyes and focus on your breathing by counting backwards five, four, three, two, one as you inhale and exhale. When you feel relaxed, imagine you are on the slopes.

Recall your favourite ski slope; see the contours of the terrain and notice the snow texture. Feel the sun on your face and the clothes you are wearing. Recreate as many sights, sounds and

feelings as you can. Feel the snow under your skis and the lateral support from your boots. Flex your ankles, feeling the pressure on your shins. Set off and link some turns. If you make an awkward turn or fall over, just edit that section by replaying the film, cutting out the imbalance and re-skiing the turn. Check your pole plant, your breathing, the rhythm of the turns.

You may find that at first you are

Imagine your favourite slope and mentally rehearse your descent

*Visualizing how you would like to
ski can help you to think positively
and add extra qualities to your skiing*

unable to 'be inside' your body, but that you can view it from the outside. Either way is useful so have a go at both. Hopefully you will find this very enjoyable and feel one hundred per cent safe. Why not visualize your ideal skier and follow them down the slope? You could even try merging with that skier for a few turns.

Take every opportunity to stock your internal movie library by watching skiing films and absorbing whole patterns of movement. Replay them internally at idle moments, while queuing at the supermarket or while travelling on public transport. People will wonder at the smile on your face and you will be surprised at the improvement you can make without a snowflake in sight.

Mental rehearsal and imagery

Once out on the slopes it is very useful to spend a little time seeing in your mind's eye the way in which you would like to ski a particular slope. See the terrain and the rhythm of the turns that you want to make. Obviously you need to be realistic about this. Imagining that you are World Champion may not perform miracles but you may add some extra qualities to what you can already do!

What qualities would you like to add to your skiing? More grace, fluidity, smoothness, control, accuracy, consistency, ease, confidence, spontaneity, commitment...? Think of something that represents the quality you are striving for – a willow, a lion, a bird, a four-wheel drive vehicle – and hold that image in your mind as you ski, allowing your body to become the image.

External and internal preparation

To achieve perfect balance on skis you need a body that is both externally and internally prepared for the task. Mountains are potentially dangerous so your clothing and equipment will need careful selection and maintenance (see Chapter 1). You may be outdoors for prolonged periods; delays in lift lines, lift malfunction or unforeseen changes in weather can turn heaven into hell. Are you well-prepared? Do you have the energy resources required to keep yourself warm and active?

Being well-prepared for activity in the mountains means being properly clothed and carefully equipped. The watchword is to be ready for any eventuality

When you ski you should not neglect your body's internal preparation. A sensible diet will help you to maintain your energy levels

Energy and diet

You will need all the energy you can get while out skiing so make sure your diet is rich in carbohydrates. Wholemeal pasta, brown rice or potatoes and wholemeal bread for dinner will top up your glycogen stores and give you slow-burning fuel for the next day. A breakfast of muesli with fresh fruit will get you going first thing. A high-energy diet consists of the following: 60% carbohydrate, 24% fat, 11% protein, 5% alcohol.

Take some dried fruit, nuts and seeds with you when you go skiing. Chocolate may be the traditional pick-me-up but the sugar high soon turns to a sugar low. Sunflower seeds, apricots and a muesli bar are a wiser choice.

Mid-week blues

Many people find that by day three of their holiday they are exhausted. Hardly surprising after travelling, adjusting to high altitude and exercising all day. Many injuries, off days and general upsets can be avoided by pacing yourself the first couple of days, stopping early or starting later to allow your glycogen energy stores to replenish rather than deplete completely.

Liquid

Through exercise and breathing in a dry atmosphere your water stores are depleted much quicker than you may expect. This, combined with excesses of white wine, cheese and coffee, means that headaches and sleeplessness are common complaints. At altitude it is extremely important to increase your intake of liquid to combat dehydration. Drink two or three glasses of water when you wake up, at lunchtime and when you get back from the slopes. Avoid coffee and wine which subtract rather than add liquid to your body, and beware of drinking spirits to warm you up. Alcohol dilates capillaries, resulting in heat loss which further reduces your core temperature.

Vive la différence

Skiing, like riding and sailing, has always included women in its competitive framework. In Alpine racing separate women's events have emerged as a result of women's physiology. Men and women differ in several ways and fair comparison is not possible where strength and power are the criteria. Although before puberty growth is approximately identical, girls forge ahead for a couple of years until the boys reach their adolescent growth spurt at about thirteen. Everything then grows about ten per cent more in boys, apart from their hips.

Surprisingly, this is structurally a great advantage for women skiers particularly when combined with fat distribution. Men have more of an inverted triangular shape with broad shoulders and narrow hips. The wider female hips and lighter upper body create a lower centre of gravity. Women in effect have a better potential ability to balance. No surprise therefore that only women perform the balance beam event in gymnastics and only men the rings.

Wider hips may mean a better base for balance but they also mean that the femur angles inwards towards the knee so that there is a tendency to be knock-kneed. Snowplough or stem movements will initially come more easily but when turning parallel the inner leg may block effective edging and leg lean. Raising awareness of the inside knee and spending more time 'educating' it to turn uphill can ease this problem.

As thigh muscles become stronger through skiing a problem may arise in the knee. As a result of the inclined femur, the angle of the quadricep muscle can pull the kneecap out of alignment and cause pain. To prevent this the parallel muscle towards the

The strength of male skiers like Peter Mueller of Switzerland lies in their power, speed and assertiveness. However, women have certain physical advantages over the men that enable them to balance better

Although women skiers are
generally more graceful than their
male counterparts, racers such as the
Swiss duo Erika Hess (below) and
Michaela Figini (bottom left) have
adopted the traditionally male
qualities of aggression and
determination to succeed

Vive la différence

inner thigh, the vastus medialis, must be strengthened to balance the quadricep development. Sit on a table with the knee flexed. Keep the ankle flexed and lift the lower leg until it is fully extended, hold, and repeat as often as possible. The last six inches of this extension are the most important. For greater effect, hang a plastic bag containing a 1kg/2lb weight from the foot and repeat the exercise.

There are some other interesting differences where women are at an advantage. Although men have a larger blood volume as well as a greater oxygen-carrying capacity within the blood itself, women appear to acclimatize to altitude better and faster than men. Although disadvantaged when exercising in the short-term, women tend to utilize fat as fuel better and dehydrate less when longer-term endurance counts. Women excel in endurance events and are more likely to survive situations of extreme deprivation.

Women are much better suited physically to survival in situations where endurance counts

Having said all that, the drop-out rate is much higher amongst women skiers. Perhaps because nearly all ski teaching has been based on an analysis of the male physique by men with men in mind. Many women in ski school feel like square pegs in round holes. Apart from the physical differences, the problems are largely due to a lack of appreciation for a difference in attitude and a need for a less competitive, more supportive learning atmosphere.

If the male qualities of strength, speed and assertiveness are de-

A useful exercise to strengthen the inner thigh is to raise and lower the legs while sitting on a table. Extra weight on your feet will increase the effectiveness

manded of a woman she may be at a loss. To be aggressive is somehow undesirable. Logical, analytical explanations may also be unsuited to women's learning patterns. They tend to be less brave than men and less willing to take risks. As little girls, they have generally not been encouraged to test the limits of their physical ability and cannot muscle their way down a ski slope when technique has broken down.

However, women bring some very special qualities to the ski slopes that have yet to be recognized and valued. Often preferring quality to quantity, the process rather than the result, they tend more easily to express grace, rhythm and whole patterns of movement. They learn effective technique quicker through greater sensitivity and body awareness.

Understanding the differences and respecting that we are neither all male nor all female will help both sexes to improve their skiing. Women need to take more risks and develop a more determined attitude, while men could learn greater sensitivity and grace.

Spending time perfecting technique without stress will pay dividends. Women need to spend extra time on less difficult slopes gaining confidence so that good technique can be relied upon on more demanding terrain.

With a lighter upper body, women often find it harder to recover once in 'the back seat', particularly if they have weak stomach muscles. The telltale sign of this is the classic hollow back problem and the 'position toilette'. By stretching and

lengthening the backs of the legs and strengthening the mid section of the body (stomach, buttocks and lower back), great improvements can be made to posture and consequently to skiing technique.

Recent developments in equipment can also help women to maximize their potential. Choosing boots with a softer ankle flex and skis with a softer front section can ease turn initiation. Fortunately, clothes are now being made for skiing rather than just looking pretty, and several brands make outfits that are both functional and fashionable.

Women tend to learn technique more quickly through greater sensitivity and body awareness, and express themselves on skis with grace and rhythm

More and more women are discovering that skiing can be fun and satisfying. Their way of skiing is different, not better or worse, just different. Recognize your strengths, value your body shape and express yourself on skis in your own way.

Chapter 7 ALL-ROUND SKIING

This chapter takes a look at a wide range of skiing activities, both competitive and recreational, old and new, and encourages competent skiers to develop their all-round ability. Whether your interest lies in cross-country skiing or slalom, downhill racing or freestyle, artificial slope skiing or mono-skiing, you can learn the necessary skills and techniques and follow the examples of the top international skiers.

Cross-country skiing

A few years ago, cross-country skiing was either considered to be the preserve of Scandinavian enthusiasts or easily mistaken for a highly energetic sport, reserved only for Olympic athletes and well outside the realms of the general recreational skier. Yet the very origins of skiing as the sport we know today are linked directly to this form of travelling over snow, propelling yourself up and down hills and across flat terrain. Using lightweight equipment with the boots fixed only at the toe, allowing the heel to move freely with each walking-sliding gait, many kilometres can be covered with the minimum of energy output.

While Alpine (downhill) skiing grew in popularity to become the major winter sport that it is today, it is only relatively recently that Nordic or cross-country skiing has seen a revival of interest. To cater for this demand by Nordic skiers, many Alpine resorts have developed special trails exclusively for cross-country skiing – from a simple 'loipe' or loop track, to a choice of trails over varied terrain and distances. Skiers wanting to get away from crowded piste-skiing or simply requiring a change of exercise, now have the chance to practise, or try out for the first time, this increasingly popular facet of the sport. Away from the bustle of a busy ski area, lift queues and packed cablecars, the reality of cross-country skiing is the pleasure of escaping into a beautiful winter landscape. Age is no barrier, it is literally a sport for all, to be undertaken anywhere there is a covering of snow that enables the skis to glide.

There are several reasons for its growth in popularity. It is an extremely safe sport in which to participate – the boots are not clamped down solid on to the ski so a fall is not impeded by the restriction of leg movement. Walkers, ramblers and climbers who wish to extend their winter activities are turning more to the use of Nordic skis as part of their weekend travels. While those who exercise through the summer – jogging and other sports – find that

One of the main attractions of cross-country skiing is the opportunity it gives you to travel through a spectacular winter landscape

Nordic skiing provides a direct follow-on for the winter months. Cross-country skiing is also considerably cheaper than Alpine skiing!

However, this upsurge of interest in Nordic skiing must be linked directly to innovations in the design of equipment, in particular of the ski sole. Traditionally associated with Nordic skiing has been the mystique of waxing techniques – the application of a grip-wax to the ski sole in order to stop the skis sliding backwards with each step. Waxes have to be selected according to the snow conditions, and it requires practice to prepare the skis correctly. Not surprisingly, would-be Nordic skiers found it tedious having to wax before every skiing session. The answer to the problem came in the form of a fish-scale pattern embossed on the middle of the ski sole. The principle of the fishscale is that it is cut into the sole like the tiles on a roof, slanting forwards so that the sharp step-edge digs into the snow if the ski slides backwards. So a simple but effective means of grip built into the ski design has revolutionized the sport. Now a skier can put on a pair of skis and set off without any of the preliminaries of waxing and ski preparation.

Cross-country racers still tend to use waxed skis for optimum performance, while non-wax soles are generally preferred by recreational skiers for their convenience

Cross-country equipment

Cross-country skis, boots and poles are much lighter than their Alpine counterparts, and for economy-conscious skiers they are also cheaper! A complete package of kit ready to take off on the snow will cost less than a pair of Alpine boots alone. Depending on the type of cross-country skiing you are going to try, there are several ski models from which to choose. Edged skis that are slightly narrower than Alpine skis are used for mountain touring; general purpose cross-country skis are normally about 52mm wide parallel cut; while training and racing skis for use in tracks are lighter and narrower in section. Most of these skis are available with non-wax (fishscale) soles, or a plain sole for the use of grip-wax. While non-wax soles are very con-

A selection of cross-country boots and poles, and a typical non-wax cross-country ski. The patterns on the ski soles may vary from model to model but they are all designed with the same aim – to allow the ski to glide forwards easily, but to stop it from sliding backwards

venient, they do lose some of the gliding efficiency of a smooth-soled ski. Hence the fact that for serious skiing, such as racing, waxed skis are still used for optimum performance. The use of laminated plastics and strong epoxy resins have made today's skis virtually unbreakable, unlike their wooden predecessors.

Because the boots are attached to the ski only at the toe, bindings are simple, light and uncomplicated. Boots need to be a snug, comfortable fit and time should be spent ensuring that no discomfort will be felt once you are out and about skiing. Boots are purchased to suit the type of binding used: the popular Nordic

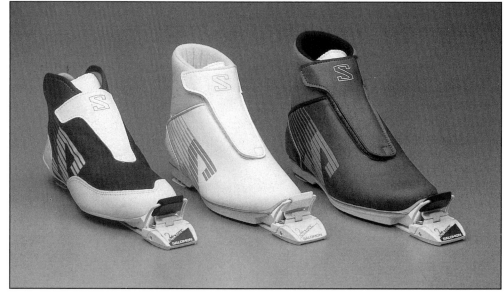

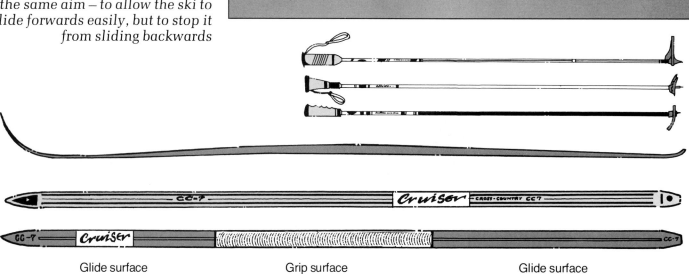

| Glide surface | Grip surface | Glide surface |

*Nordic racers in typical gear,
holding their skis aloft in jubilation.
Both skis and poles are longer than
their Alpine counterparts*

norm 75mm and 50mm width bindings allow for a wide selection of different types of boot; while other special designs of bindings are only compatible with that particular manufacturer's boot model. Poles are a necessary part of cross-country technique, and need to be long enough to aid the forward stride and glide movements. They are therefore designed to give a snug hand grip and drag-free snow basket. Robust light alloy poles will give all-round service, whether you intend to do touring or competitive skiing.

The choice of clothing depends to a great extent on the type of cross-country skiing undertaken. Ideal is quality thermal underwear that allows the body to breathe, with thin layers of T-shirts, sweaters or windcheaters. Wear narrow tracksuit bottoms or lightweight stretch knickerbockers until you require the specialized one-piece suits as used by the connoisseurs. One pair of warm socks will be enough, with mittens being ideal for touring. However, if you aspire to serious technique, then lightweight gloves give a better feel to pole use. Heat loss is a constant factor in any cold weather activity, so wear a hat that covers the ears – if you get too hot you can always take it off or strip off one of the layers! Because of the action involved in Nordic skiing, your clothing should allow for arm-stretching movements. A lightweight wind or rainproof jacket and overtrousers complete the wardrobe. Salopettes, as used for Alpine skiing, are fine for general ski wandering, but bulky ski jackets can be too warm and cumbersome.

Cross-country technique

In simple terms, if you can walk you can cross-country ski; you do not have to be super fit, and you can have a go irrespective of age. However, in order to enjoy cross-country skiing to its fullest extent, you will have to learn the basic techniques, and it is strongly recommended that you join a ski class under a qualified instructor.

In its simplest form, cross-country technique is quite straightforward. It involves walking on skis and most people find it easier to learn than Alpine technique

Two-phase or diagonal stride

This is the fundamental action by which you can propel yourself across the snow. The natural walking movements are extended to enable a forward gliding momentum over flat ground and up easy gradients. The leg and ski are 'kicked' forwards with each stride to obtain a short slide from ski to ski, helped by a push off the opposite pole plant. Tracks made in the snow will guide the skis with each slide forwards, leaving the skier to concentrate on balance and the timing of arm and leg movements. The sequence of leg stride and arm swing should be unhurried; you should concentrate on finding a smooth rhythm that gives a short glide forwards with each step. It needs a little practice, but you will soon find how little effort is required to cover the ground.

Double poling

To rest the leg strides on the flat, and when descending slight inclines, forward momentum can be maintained by simply pushing with both poles. The arms are extended forwards with the upper body erect, the poles planted slightly angled backwards. By bending the upper body forwards and down, pushing on the poles at the same time, you can follow the thrust forwards by continuing to push on the poles with your arms until they are stretched out to the rear. The movements should again be performed smoothly to get the benefit of a maximum glide forwards.

Cross-country technique

Step or skate turns

In order to change direction when a sharp turn in the track appears, or when an obstacle is in the way, the skis are stepped out to the side. The two-phase striding action is adapted to a step sideways and forwards, altering the line of direction of the inside ski into the turn. The outside ski is stepped in parallel, and then successive steps are continued until the new direction has been reached. Initially it is easier to take only small angled steps to the side, but, with practice, more vigorous 'skating' glides can be obtained by pushing off the outside ski.

The ski pole is an important aspect of cross-country technique. Poles need to be sufficiently long to assist the skier's forward glide and slide movements

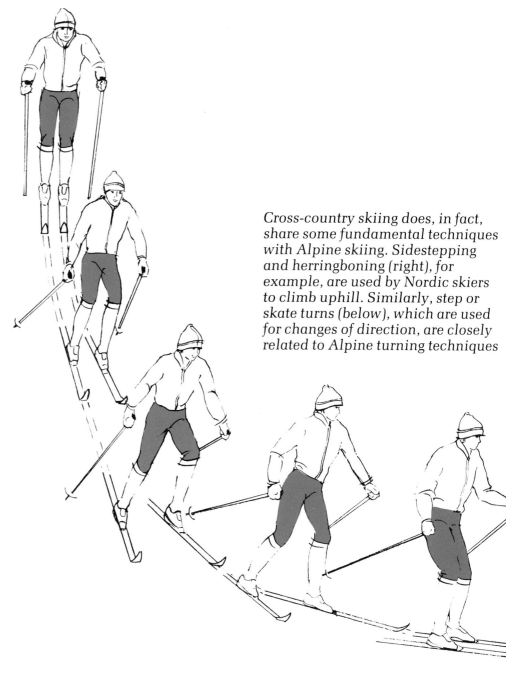

Cross-country skiing does, in fact, share some fundamental techniques with Alpine skiing. Sidestepping and herringboning (right), for example, are used by Nordic skiers to climb uphill. Similarly, step or skate turns (below), which are used for changes of direction, are closely related to Alpine turning techniques

Climbing uphill

This requires a shortening of the stride and pole action in order to maintain a grip on the snow and good push on the poles. If it is too steep for the skis to hold a grip, then they can be angled out and the herringbone step used (see Chapter 2). For controlling descents, the snowplough as used in Alpine technique will keep the brakes on and enable turns to be steered by shifting weight on to the outer ski. Because the skis are longer than Alpine skis, the snowplough angle will be larger, and a little more feeling for edging the skis on the inside of the foot is required.

Telemark skiing

In the 1860s Sondre Norheim, a Norwegian ski jumper, invented the first ski turn. He needed a way to come to a halt after jumping and the Telemark turn, named after the region in which he lived, served his purpose. It was later adapted by Alpine downhill skiers and, with the introduction of heel hold bindings, evolved into the stem christiania, the predecessor of modern parallel turns.

Telemark turns are done with free heel bindings. The 'classic' position where the skier allows the inside ski to trail behind by dropping the knee effectively elongates the base of support and stabilizes the fore-aft balance – a problem created by lack of heel hold on a downhill descent.

The Telemark revival began in the 1970s in North America with growing numbers of people going 'back-country' skiing. The cumbersome European Alpine touring equipment of downhill skis and boots adapted for climbing and skiing steep slopes did not suit their gentler, rolling hills and style of winter backpacking.

Their terrain demanded lighter but durable cross-country equipment. Taking advantage of the resilience of fibreglass, cross-country skis were adapted for downhill descents. The modern Telemark ski is slightly wider than a Nordic ski and has metal edges. Three-pin bail operated bindings fit the 75mm (Nordic norm) Telemark boots. Made of leather, the boots give lateral support for turning but allow enough flex at the ball of the foot for the kick and glide cross-country movement and the Telemark turn.

It was not long before the Telemark skiers found that their equipment worked just as well on piste and the Telemark revolution hit the slopes. It is possible to do regular parallel turns on the equipment and many people start this way to build confidence before attempting the classic Telemark turn. The lightness of the equipment and grace of the movements appeal to many skiers, as well as the ease with which you can get far from the madding crowd and walk uphill with the addition of adhesive skins.

Slalom and giant slalom races have been held since the 1970s in North America and have recently sprung up in Europe. Surprisingly stable at very high speeds these racers have adapted the classic low Telemark position into a more dynamic shape where the feet are closer together and both skis are almost evenly weighted. Although not as stable on ice, steep or mogulled slopes pose no problems for

The classic Telemark turn

those who use this type of turn.

Once equipped, start off by doing parallel or snowplough turns. You will find little fore-aft stability so practise dropping the uphill knee while in a traverse. This effectively lengthens your base support and lowers your body mass.

To start a turn from a shallow traverse, begin in a narrow plough and slide the upper ski forwards ahead of the downhill (inside) ski. As you enter the fall line your weight should be evenly distributed and both skis should be on their inside edges. As the turn progresses, the inner knee should roll over to flatten the ski and the completion of the turn should be made almost parallel, using the edges of both skis. There may be slightly more weight on the downhill ski at this point. The upper body should remain facing the direction of momentum throughout as the legs rotate allowing for appropriate angulation. This anticipation will assist in the initiation of the next turn. To link turns the upper ski should move forwards and 'feather' out into a narrow plough before sliding forwards as above. With practice, linked short swing turns can be made in the fall line.

After more than 100 years, Sondre Norheim must be smiling at the renaissance of his ski turn.

The Telemark turn is distinctive for its 'dropped-knee' position, with the inside ski trailing behind and the outside ski leading

Snowboarding

Many sliding and rolling sports have crossbred or incorporated new mechanisms in recent times. Think of windsurfing (sailing × surfing), skateboarding (surfing × roller-skating), land-yachting or grass-skiing. Snow-surfing is but another recent hybrid. The potential for surfing down powder slopes is now a reality; at one time it was just a dream of the beachboys of Hawaii, California and Australia. Many a snow surfboard was crafted out of plywood in garage workshops over the years.

During the 1970s and 1980s amateur invention gave way to serious design and notable development work was undertaken by a company called Winterstick in Salt Lake City, USA. The inventor and manufacturer of the Winterstick, Dimitrije Milovich, spent six years shaping and equipping his deck with the right turning properties.

Unfortunately many American ski resorts would have none of it. Snowboarders, who had to carry their decks on and off chairlifts and who chose to ski unpatrolled areas of the mountain, were banned. The Winterstick went out of production for a while. As with the monoski, it was the French who decided to liberalize their mountains to snowboarders and try their hands at developing the equipment.

Snowboarding is now enjoying a revival of enthusiasm on both sides of the Atlantic and the decks are incorporating new features which make them easier to use: steel edges that protrude slightly from the base surface for extra grip on piste and 'bind-

ings' (in the form of plastic boot shells screwed to the deck) which provide greater leverage for turning. Significantly, a release binding is currently under development.

Potentially, snowboarding has a lot to offer anyone who likes 'alternative' sports. The surfer, or skateboarder, who is normally restricted to riding a short-lived wave or hill, can enjoy several miles of continuous downhill riding, with short breaks to gain the necessary uplift. By wearing a pair of mini-skis the board can even be carried uphill on a draglift.

Snowboarding itself is now crossbreeding to form other variants. The

Snowboarding combines the exhilaration of surfing with the thrill of riding down the mountain

Swingbo is a deck with a steering mechanism linked to two skis underneath that steer when the deck is tilted. Windsurf sails are also being mounted on snowboards for extra thrills. The sail can either be used for forward thrust on flat areas of snow or it can be used for its braking properties on long, wide downhill stretches such as glaciers.

Snowboarding, in short, is currently the most significant area of design development in snow-related sports.

Monoskiing

Waterskiers like to monoski at an early stage of learning, so it might seem logical that monoskiing should be the predominant form of snow skiing. Monoskiing on snow is, however, a recent phenomenon and a specialized interest. The invention of a former champion surfer, Mike 'Micky' Doyle, monoskiing first gained publicity in American ski films in the mid 1970s. Prior to this, anyone who wanted to ski on one ski had to mount a T-shaped metal platform (with two sets of bindings) above a normal ski.

Doyle could not accept this compromise and started from scratch. He wanted a ski that would offer something of the thrill of surfing down a mountain. He formed a partnership with a Californian surfboard manufacturer, Bahne, and several hundred wide monoskis were made. Their construction included an aluminium honeycomb core and the design pre-empted that used on most monoskis today: tapered sides that end with a narrow point at the tail (rather than at the central 'waist' of a normal ski).

It was the French who fully capitalized on the idea several years later and there are now a number of large ski factories in France making monoskis.

The enthusiasm for monoskiing is far from a gimmick-led craze. A monoski has two distinct mechanical advantages over a pair of skis: its surface area, which is equivalent to nearly three skis, and the fact that both feet turn and tilt the board together.

The surface area of the ski fills the space that would normally be a gap between two skis. The skier's weight is spread over this broader area and the ski therefore floats more buoyantly in deep snow. This is an advantage not only in powder, where the thrill of banked turns is considerable, but in spring snow and slush, where the ski suffers less drag from the suction.

Although many people monoski on piste and through mogul fields, there are no particular advantages of the design in these conditions. The monoski should really be regarded as a means to freedom and access into snow conditions that might otherwise be disconcerting.

How easy is it to learn? Monoskiing, whatever the myths, is essentially a variant on standard technique: the ski does exactly the same job in a slightly different way. Having your skis locked together means, firstly, that balance is reduced. Keep your arms a little wider to compen-

Monoskiing allows you the freedom to explore new and different terrain

sate. Gentle bumps help the ski turn by unweighting it as you go over the rise, so spend your first day on this type of terrain. Keep the ski turning in and out of the fall line to build up the rhythm and make your pole planting positive – it is even more of an aid to timing than it is on two skis.

Traversing needs a fresh approach because the upper foot cannot slide forwards as it would normally. The 'square feet' position on a monoski can lead to the ski skidding away at the tail. Avoid this by twisting your upper body strongly so that it faces down the mountain even more obviously than it would usually.

Stick with it! Monoskiing is tiring at first and takes a few days to master. If it works for you, you will probably not want to return to two skis for powder skiing – the exhilaration is immense.

Giant slalom

In many ways the toughest of the four Alpine disciplines, the giant slalom tests the racers' highly-developed technique, as well as their physical strength. Ingemar Stenmark makes it look extremely easy as he carves smooth, tight turns, keeping the skis on edge even when the snow is rock hard. Yet to achieve his beautiful style he has developed the body of an athlete.

Originally introduced after the Second World War to enable the resorts with smaller mountains to be able to run an alternative, higher speed event to the slalom, giant slalom eventually became so highly controlled that the speed and variation in terrain disappeared. With two runs over different courses, which are just over one kilometre long dropping over 300 metres, with fifty five gates, this event has almost become the modern form of slalom. Although perhaps not quite as entertaining for the public as the other events, giant slalom is very demanding on the racers. The energy they use up mastering the tough directional changes is high, and, moreover, they must race twice in one day.

Giant slalom racers wear a tight aerodynamic suit, like the downhill racers, but with some padding to protect themselves against hitting the gates at high speed. The skis are usually 5cm longer than slalom skis, but not as long as downhill skis. A giant slalom ski has to be stable to carve a smooth round turn, even on the hardest and roughest of icy slopes, and yet generate additional acceleration out of the turn to win more speed.

The length of the courses results in fitness playing a particularly influential role. In addition to this, the good giant slalom racer needs finesse, precision and good 'feel' to maintain speed through the sometimes steep terrain and sharp corners.

Giant slalom is in many ways the most challenging of the World Cup disciplines. Markus Wasmaier of West Germany combines speed and technique to tackle the Crans-Montana course in the 1987 World Championships

This sequence shows Maria Walliser of Switzerland in the giant slalom. Notice how she turns well in advance of the next gate so that she can keep to a good line down the course

Slalom

Although the shortest of the four World Cup events, slalom is probably the most exacting. With racers charging down steep icy slopes, around spring-loaded plastic gates firmly planted in the snow, fractions of centimetres can separate a skier from being in or out of the course.

The competitors have two runs, with up to seventy five gates for the men and sixty gates for the women to negotiate. The times of the two runs are added together to find the overall winner. The racers must pass between the alternating blue and red gates which weave down the mountainside. The course is studied before the race to determine the fastest line, although no practice is allowed on the run.

With the fastest line being the shortest, the racers strive to get as close to the gates as possible. This results in quite heavy impact with the poles, hence the development of padded sweaters, trousers, and gloves. The recent introduction of the spring-loaded pole has changed slalom skiing style. The lines have become even shorter because the racer does not need to ski round the poles – they deflect out of the way of the skier on contact.

This change has removed some of the precise style from the event and replaced it with a more dramatic explosive action, which has narrowed down even further the margin for error. It has also resulted in the competitors looking more like American Football players. A slalom racer now stands in the starting hut with a helmet, and wearing strong padding down the arms, knees and thighs and gloves that would look more at home in a boxing ring. Slalom skis are the shortest that a racer will ski on, and normally have razor-sharp edges to grip on the steep icy hills. The skis are specially designed to give the maximum possible edge grip, yet have a very quick edge rebound, so that the skis turn quickly.

With up to 100 racers negotiating the first run, the courses have to be very well prepared. The racers like them to be rock hard and icy so that they stand up to all the sharp edges cutting over them. In the World Cup, only the fastest thirty are allowed to start the second run; the quickest fifteen skiers are reversed, with the leading racer going fifteenth.

Slalom is one of the most entertaining and exciting of the disciplines for the spectator – just watch Bojan Krizaj carving quick turns down the steep Wengen slope with the gates flying about in his wake. For the racer, however, it can be one of the most frustrating; not only are there just hundredths of a second separating the top racers, but there is also very little between being in or out of the demanding courses.

Andreas Wenzel of Liechtenstein demonstrates how the spring-loaded slalom poles deflect out of the way

Super-G

The super-G is the newest of the disciplines and was introduced to the circuit with the idea of giving the downhill racers more of a chance to collect World Cup points in the technical disciplines. The super-G is a one-run race, shorter than a downhill, yet longer than the giant slalom. The course is set so that the speed is higher than the more established giant slalom, with a few jumps and exciting turns built in to entertain the public as well as challenge the racers.

This new event is in fact a re-introduction of the original giant slalom, which had changed its character so dramatically over the preceding twenty years that it had become a discipline more akin to the specialized slalom.

The event is still struggling to achieve full acceptance by the World Cup racers – the great Mahre twins and Ingemar Stenmark refused to participate in it. Its success is very much dependent on the imagination of the trainer setting the course. When first introduced to the World Championships in Crans-Montana in 1987, the terrain was so steep and sufficiently monotonous that the super-G more closely resembled a giant slalom than the high-speed, entertaining test that officials were hoping for. Yet many of the World Cup races are run on the lower sections of downhill courses which offer a good variety of terrain.

The courses are set on runs about two kilometres long and dropping 600 metres down the mountainside. Approximately thirty five gates are then carefully placed for the racers to negotiate. Super-G racers wear a tight one-piece suit, and lightweight hel-

mets are compulsory due to the high speeds reached. The skis are the same length or longer than giant slalom skis, and are designed to be very fast and quiet through the long turns.

With no practice allowed and skiers hitting speeds of one hundred kilometres an hour, the excitement for the racers lies in handling the sudden changes in the terrain and the pattern of the course, while main-

Peter Mueller of Switzerland competing in the super-G strives to control his turns at maximum speed on icy terrain

taining their momentum without catching too much aerodynamic drag. When watching Markus Wasmaier flow smoothly down through the gates it is hard to appreciate the speed at which he is travelling.

Downhill racing

Downhill racing is the blue ribband event on the circuit. Not only is it very simple to understand – the winner is the fastest person out of the starting hut, down the mountain and through the finish – but, with the high speeds involved, it is the most entertaining. Originally a straight race down the mountainside, downhill developed over the years into its present form, having adjusted to the increased speeds of the competitors and the latest developments in equipment and training methods.

The men's courses are usually three to four kilometres long, and snake their way down vertical drops of between 800 to 1000 metres. The women's courses tend to be a little shorter and with slightly less vertical drop.

With racers travelling at such high speeds, safety has become an important issue to course designers; control gates, safety nets and fences are all now part of every course. New courses are carefully mapped out and inspected to ensure that the necessary safety requirements have been met. This has the effect of restricting the course designer somewhat, so that it is difficult now to develop new courses with the same memorable character as the classics – the famous Streiff in Kitzbühel or the Lauberhorn in Wengen. These challenging mountainsides were raced on long before rules to enhance the safety of the sport were established.

Sections like the Mausefalle in Kitzbühel and the Wasserstation in Wengen do not meet exactly the modern definition of the rules regarding width of piste, but their tradition is greater. However, new courses like at Bormio in Italy and at Whistler, Canada, have been designed with such care and imagination that the spectacle and safety have been maintained while keeping the racers tested to the full. There has also been the occasional downhill course that met the necessary rules and regulations but lacked the terrain to bring the best out of the racers. The Olympic downhills of Lake Placid and Sarajevo are two such courses. Lake Placid started off with some tight icy corners, but the speed was fairly low. It was not until further down that the speed increased, although the course had become straight and flat. In Sarajevo, by building a number of jumps, they disguised the flatness of the course which favoured the gliders on the circuit.

There are two basic separate requirements of a downhill depending on the layout. The flatter sections of the course will favour the gliders, the skiers who have a good aerodynamic tuck and who can let their skis run well, like Peter Mueller. Then there are the technical courses that favour racers such as Pirmin Zurbriggen who can accelerate better out of the turns. The good courses will have both types of section but some, like Crans-Montana, have more gliding sections broken up by some large jumps to

Bill Johnson (USA) in action

enhance the mental challenge and entertain the spectators.

Each racer should have at least three training runs on the course before the race where possible. Also, the teams spend time on the course discussing training runs, analysing the lines to find the fastest way down, and memorizing each centimetre of the course so that in the race their thoughts are fully concentrated on going fast. Downhill racing is comparable to the Grand Prix motor racing circuit where the equipment is a contributing factor to a racer's success. Tests are made during the training sessions to ensure that the skis are sliding as fast as possible for the conditions. Changes in conditions can upset even the most careful of preparations, and victories can depend on ski soles, just as tyres affect the performance of racing cars.

Races last from one minute forty five seconds to two minutes thirty seconds for the longest course (the Lauberhorn in Wengen). The racers need extreme physical fitness to cope with the demands of the course and to maintain as low a position as possible to reduce aerodynamic resistance. This explains the huge thigh muscles the competitors develop.

With hundredths of seconds separating racers in all the disciplines, perfect preparation is vital. They must pay attention to the physical, mental and technical aspects of their racing as well as to their equipment. A year-round programme is undertaken by each of the competing nations to ensure that their racers are the ones standing on the victory rostrum at the end of the day.

Freestyle

The first international competitions held in the United States in the 1960s were considered by many as 'crazy', and a surfing term was used to describe the madcap descents of these 'hotdoggers'. Fortunately, the sport has outgrown this name and the original single descent, where anything went and recoveries were marked high, has developed into a three event sport: the mogul event, the ballet event and the aerial event.

Freestyle is the youngest member of the FIS (International Ski Federation) family of competitive skiing sports, having only been officially adopted in 1981. It has been granted demonstration status at the 1988 Winter Olympics and is likely to become a fully-fledged Olympic medal event in 1992.

A skier may specialize in a single event or compete in all three for a combined result. The current Combined World Champions Alain Laroche from Canada and Conny Kissling from Switzerland demonstrate strength and versatility by consistently reaching the finals in all three events and usually finishing in the top five.

To be an expert skier you need to be versatile and athletic, and there is no doubt that learning basic freestyle ballet and mogul skiing will improve your balance, edge awareness and ability to respond to a variety of different situations.

Freestyle skiing is both dramatic and graceful, and capitalizes on the skier's ability to combine strength, agility and versatility

The mogul event

The mogul event entails fall line skiing on a steep, heavily mogulled course, and the competitors are judged for the quality of their turns, their jumping skill and their speed. A good run is one in which the skier balances on the knife edge of maximum speed and technical control.

The skier must turn rhythmically, without deviating from the fall line and with continuous ski-snow contact – except of course when performing jumps. The upper body faces downhill, naturally anticipating each turn. The skier must absorb the terrain with the lower body, through hip, knee and ankle flexion and extension. The arms and shoulders remain quiet, only making essential pole planting movements.

As a skier you are probably no stranger to moguls (see Chapter 5). There is no doubt that traversing a mogul slope can be an uncomfortable ride. Moguls need to be skied in the fall line, so practise controlled fall line skiing on smooth slopes, without moguls first. Skiing in new snow will also help you to understand how moguls are formed and how to pick a good line. Many people view moguls as enemies – make them your friend.

Specialist mogul equipment
Competitive mogul skiing requires a high performance ski with slalom side cut. The FIS ruling for minimum adult ski lengths is 190cm for men and 180cm for women. Generally the taller, heavier skiers exceed these lengths by 5-10cm, and shorter, lighter skiers (like the Japanese, for example) are permitted to use a shorter length.

Philippe Deiber of France performing a spread eagle jump in the mogul event. Twenty five per cent of the marks are allotted to jumps

The aerial event

The aerial competition consists of two different jumps performed off a prepared 'kicker' and these are judged on takeoff, height, distance, style, precision and landing. The aerial site is made up of an inrun, jump table, 'knoll' and steep landing hill (minimum thirty seven degrees). Several jumps are constructed according to exact specifications to suit the amount of 'air time' required.

In particular the judges reward the skier's ability to balance a maximum degree of difficulty with excellence of execution. A well-executed jump can beat a less perfect performance of a more difficult manoeuvre. The current (1986) Men's World Aerial Champion, Lloyd Langlois, a diminutive French Canadian, is famous for his ability to combine somersaults and twists. He performed a triple twisting triple somersault to clinch the title.

Warning! Freestyle aerials are potentially dangerous if attempted without expert guidance. It takes careful training to become a top freestyler and several activities provide valuable foundation training: gymnastics, classical ballet, contemporary dance, ice skating, trampolining and diving.

To begin aerials, do some 'dry land' jumps first of all. Practise jumping up in the air without ski boots and lifting your arms in front. Spring off your toes and absorb the landing by flexing ankles, knees and hips. See if you can land quietly! Upright aerials can then be learned off small bumps but make sure you have chosen a site out of the way of other skiers. Check that the landing area is sloping (at least

twenty five degrees) and free of foreign objects. Start with a short inrun in order to get a feel for the takeoff, and then progress gradually. To jump well you need to be aware of differences in inrun speed (which can change dramatically from hour to hour), 'pop' (extension) on takeoff, form in the air and landing so that you absorb any shocks and can ski away in balance.

Somersaults should only be performed on a properly controlled jump site with qualified personnel in attendance. If you want to learn inverted aerials, you must first learn some 'air sense' by doing upright jumps and then join a trampoline club to learn the rudiments of bouncing safely, and eventually progress to somersaults. It is then essential to

An aerial jump site showing 'kickers' (above). Mike Whealey (right), Europa Cup Champion in 1984, was the first British skier to jump triples

practise on a water jump in summer before attempting any somersaults on snow. There are special training centres in Europe and North America, so contact your national governing body for details.

Specialist aerial equipment

Skis are between 160-175cm with a stiff tail to withstand the force of landing. The bindings may be mounted slightly forwards to provide further landing stability. Ski sticks are only used in upright aerials. Helmets are mandatory except under very special circumstances.

The ballet event

The ballet event consists of a 2½-minute performance on gentle terrain which is choreographed to music. The performance includes a balanced programme of spins, steps, jumps and somersaults and points are awarded for technical difficulty, choreography and overall performance.

When awarding marks the judges take into account the technical difficulty of each manoeuvre, which is classified and the quality of its execution evaluated. A balance between artistry and athleticism must be struck while interpreting the mood of the music through original linking manoeuvres and bodily expression. The quality and elegance of the skier's carriage and ease of movement must be apparent, showing balletic posture and grace. Jan Bucher from the United States, the 1986 World Champion, has dominated women's ballet for the past five years. Her strength lies in her clean in-air rotations (axels) and sophisticated choreography gained from years of competitive figure skating.

Unless you equip yourself with shorter skis there is a limit to what you can achieve safely. However, learning to ski on the outside edges is a very valuable asset for improving your balance, especially when caught on the 'wrong' foot.

1 Start by traversing on the uphill ski.
2 On a shallow slope in the fall line, hop on to the outside edge and ride the ski into the traverse. It will become the uphill ski.
3 Once you feel comfortable doing that, hop on to the outside edge down the fall line and steer it into the opposite traverse. Feel your little toe pressing the edge into the snow and press your shin into the front of your boot to help you steer. Balancing with the arms, hold the free leg straight out and back.
4 Once you have mastered balancing and turning on the 'outside edge' lift your free leg higher and you will be doing a royale christie.

The ballet event is probably the most 'artistic' of the freestyle events. In addition to originality and elegance, the competitors must also display strength and athleticism

360° spin

It is likely that you have done the occasional involuntary spin on skis. Learning to do them intentionally will improve your co-ordination and edge awareness

1 *Practise a narrow backwards snowplough on a gentle slope, keeping your bottom well tucked in*
2 *If you look over your shoulder you will start a backwards snowplough turn*
3 *Once you have allowed this to continue across the fall line you simply transfer your weight and ski forwards again*
4 *Now make a turn uphill adding on the backwards turn you did in points 2 and 3 above*

Specialist ballet equipment

You will need special ballet skis or a strong junior slalom ski. The minimum ski length allowed in ballet is eighty one per cent of body height. Ski poles are much longer than normal to assist in maintaining balletic posture and in performing axels and pole flips. A small cassette player with earphones is used for practising with the music.

Artificial slope skiing

The original concept of an artificial ski slope arose from the need to give newcomers to the sport an opportunity to try out the equipment and learn a few basic techniques without the need to travel and incur vast expense and in the security of a controlled environment. As interest in the activity grew a number of slopes developed beyond the original concept into mini ski resorts in their own right. Although all the slopes offer skiing tuition the larger ones are also able to offer recreational skiing. During off-peak times, many of these larger slopes run competitions and fun events where the average recreational skier can experience ski racing for the first time. In fact, many of the British team members over the past fifteen years began their racing careers on artificial slopes.

The two most common questions prospective skiers ask about artificial slopes are: 'Is it like snow?' and 'If I learn on the plastic, will I be able to do it on the snow?'

The answer to the second question is yes. Once you have learned to ski on the plastic, the conversion to snow skiing is a very straightforward and indeed pleasant process.

The first question, however, is not so easy to answer. Of course an artificial slope cannot be exactly like snow, but from the point of view of ski technique it does act like snow.

So, what are artificial slopes made of? There are throughout the world various different artificial skiing surfaces. Broadly speaking, they can be categorized as one of two types: plastic injected spikes or nylon bristle. Both work or perform technically in

the same way except that the bristle variety tends to simulate the feel of snow more realistically. Popular opinion has dictated that, in Britain at least, the majority of the larger slopes are constructed with the bristle type of surface. It is favoured by experienced skiers, racers will race on nothing else except snow and ski instructors prefer it to any of the plastic injection varieties.

The main noticeable difference between the real thing and plastic lies in the fact that snow provides a more slippery surface. Snow is very slippery, whereas the amount of friction between the skis and any artificial surface means that the skis tend not to slide so well. All the slopes over the years have used lubricants to overcome this problem and, during the last five years, many have installed water sprinkler systems to keep the skiing surface wet. Installing such systems means better skiing for the customer and far less damage to both

The controlled environment of an artificial ski slope is the ideal place to acquire and practise new skills – you can have fun, too!

skis and the surface for the operators. A well-designed, lubricated slope, even in the middle of summer, should now still be acceptably slippery.

Many competent skiers tend to class artificial slope skiing as second rate. This is mainly due to the fact that they are unable to recognize the advantages of using one. In terms of learning technique an artificial slope provides an ideal environment. You should consider it as a classroom, free from the sometimes unhelpful factors that can affect your ski technique on a mountainside. Perhaps the biggest advantage of artificial slopes, though, is that they afford skiers the opportunity of practising all year round. Use them to improve your skiing so that you can enjoy your holiday to the full.

Speed skiing

The quest to be fastest over a given distance is not unusual in sport. But in skiing it is something special.

In the 'Flying Kilometre', or 'KL' (Kilometre Lance), speed skiers travel faster than any other unpowered human being on earth – their only fuel is gravity. To achieve the highest possible speeds they ski a straight course with a gradient of forty to sixty degrees and use several special items of equipment.

Speed skis are up to 240cm long but they are connected to normal boots and bindings (with special stiff competition springs). Skintight suits and elongated helmets are used to reduce wind resistance and turbulence to a minimum.

By deploying this equipment, speed skiers travel at least fifty per cent faster than downhill racers. They are at the limits of control and balance, and thorough safety measures are very important. The track must be carefully prepared, with smooth changes of gradient, as little camber as possible and a consistent surface. The snow has to be side-stepped by the competitors before an event starts and the camber is sometimes checked by rolling a balloon filled with water from the top. The balloon's path will define the fall line and if the course veers from this it might be dangerous.

Competitors train for the KL by practising their tucks in the kind of wind tunnels used by car and aircraft designers. Relevant speed skiing data (height, gradient and so on) can be fed into the tunnel's computer to provide an estimated speed for a given track. However, real experience on the mountain cannot be simulated. Weightlifting and fitness training are essential to compete seriously since the stresses of skiing over 100mph are considerable.

The KL has its roots in competitions organized in St Moritz (Switzerland) in the early 1930s and most world records between 1945 and 1975 were set in Cervinia (Italy).

The typical gear and tuck position of the speed skier

Speeds above 200kph (124mph) have been seen at Portillo (Chile), Silverton (USA), Les Arcs and La Clusaz (France). A new world record of 212.50kph (132.06mph) was set by Graham Wilkie of Great Britain in Les Arcs in April 1987.

Glossary

Aerial event
A freestyle competition of two different jumps performed off a prepared 'kicker'. Competitors are judged on takeoff, height, style, precision and landing.

Angulation
The term used to describe the shape of the body as it is bent forwards at the hips and the legs are bent forwards and inwards to edge the skis. There are three types of angulation: knee, hip and knee-hip.

Anti-friction plate
Part of the toe piece of the binding, which is designed to reduce friction between boot and ski.

Artificial slope skiing
Skiing on an artificial surface made from plastic injected spikes or nylon bristle.

Avalanche
The sudden slide downhill of a large mass of snow, ice and other materials.

Axels
Freestyle ballet jumps where the skier completes one and a half or two and a half rotations in the air around a vertical axis.

Backscratcher
An upright freestyle jump where the knees bend so that the skis are vertical and the arms lift over the head.

Ballet event
A freestyle discipline comprising a two-and-a-half minute performance, which includes spins, steps, jumps and somersaults, usually choreographed to music. Points are awarded for technical difficulty, choreography and overall performance.

Banking
Inclining the entire body, or mainly the hips, to the inside of a turn in order to keep the skis edged.

Basic swings
Swings which combine traversing, snowploughing and sideslipping. They are initiated in the plough position and are linked by a short traverse.

Basket
The small metal or plastic disc near the tip of a ski pole that stops the pole sinking too far into the snow.

Binding
The device, usually comprising a separate toe piece and heel piece, which fits on to the ski and holds the boot in place.

Bumps see *Moguls*

Button lift
Also known as a 'Poma' lift, a button lift comprises long metal poles or cables that are attached to a moving cable and have small round 'seats' at the end so that skiers may be transported uphill.

Cablecar
Built to span substantial changes in altitude, the cablecar is a large cabin suspended from a moving cable.

Camber
The term given to the arch a ski forms when lying flat on an even surface. Its function is to distribute the skier's weight evenly along the running surface of the ski.

Carving
Utilizing ski design to turn with a minimum of skidding.

Centrifugal force
The opposite of centripetal force, centrifugal force throws a body outwards when pivoting around a central point.

Centripetal force
The external force which, together with snow resistance, makes the skis turn around a central point due to their design.

Chairlift
A ski lift which transports skiers uphill on seats suspended from a moving cable.

Compression
The loading of the body caused by changes in terrain.

Cossack
A freestyle spread eagle jump in a piked position.

Diagonal sidestepping
The same as sidestepping except that the skis are stepped forwards as well as uphill.

Double poling
A technique used in both Alpine and cross-country skiing to achieve forward propulsion by planting both ski poles together and pushing off from them.

Downhill racing
One of the four Alpine World Cup disciplines. Competitors race down a specially designed course that must meet strict safety standards.

Downsinking
Flexing down in the ankles, knees and hip joints to achieve a low position.

Draglifts
There are two main types: T-bars and button lifts. They transport skiers uphill while wearing their skis.

Dry slope skiing see *Artificial slope skiing*

Dynamic balance
The opposite of static balance, dynamic balance is achieved by adopting a body

shape that allows active and effective movement to cope with external forces and changes in terrain, and is closely linked to the ready position and the skier's ability to match his skis to the terrain.

Extension
Rising up in the ankles, knees and hip joints.

Fall line
The quickest and shortest route down a slope.

Flat light
Poor visibility, making it difficult to judge distances and differences in terrain.

Flex
The term given to the bending characteristics of a ski or boot.

Flexion
The action of bending, either upwards or downwards, in the ankles, knees and hip joints.

Flight plan
The statement of the details of a proposed freestyle aerial manoeuvre.

Flip
An alternative term for a somersault.

Floater
The jump designed specifically for upright aerials.

Flying Kilometre see Speed skiing

Freestyle
Consisting of three events – ballet, moguls and aerials – freestyle is the youngest member of the FIS family of competitive skiing.

Giant slalom
A cross between slalom and downhill, giant slalom is one of the four World Cup disciplines. The course is designed with specially positioned gates and the event is a test of the competitors' speed and turning techniques.

GLM
Graduated Length Method – the American version of Ski évolutif.

Gravity
The force which pulls a body towards the centre of the earth. Skis slide downhill due to gravity.

Grip-wax
The wax applied to the soles of cross-country skis to make them grip the snow, particularly when pushing off or climbing uphill.

Heel piece
The part of the binding that holds the back of the boot in place on the ski.

Helicopter
An upright freestyle jump with a 360° or 720° rotation around a vertical axis.

Herringbone step
The technique used to climb short, easy slopes. The skis are placed in an open scissor position and stepped uphill.

Inertia
The term describing a body, either stationary or in uniform motion, which is not being acted upon by an external force.

Initiation phase
The phase of the turn in which the skier begins to move his skis into the new direction of travel.

Inner boot
The soft lining which fits inside the

plastic shell of the ski boot and which is removable.

Kick turn
A method of turning around on the flat whereby one ski is lifted and turned on its tail through 180°. The other ski is then brought alongside the first. However, this turn can be dangerous and is *not* recommended for novices.

Kicker
The jump(s) designed for inverted freestyle aerials.

Langlauf
The German term for Nordic cross-country skiing.

Layout
A straight body position in a freestyle somersault.

Line
The route taken by a mogul skier through the bumps. Also, the route taken by skiers down a race course.

Loipe
A specially prepared track for Nordic cross-country skiing.

Moguls
Mounds of hard packed snow created by skiers' turns, also known as bumps.

Mogul event
A freestyle discipline which entails fall line skiing on a steep, mogulled course. Competitors are judged on the quality of their turns, their jumping skill and speed.

Monoskiing
An alternative form of skiing where one broader ski replaces the normal two.

Moving mountain
A machine comprising a revolving carpet

Glossary

which some ski shops have installed to enable skiers to try out new boots.

Mule kick
The same as a backscratcher except that the skis are held to the side of the body.

Non-wax skis
Cross-country skis with a pattern embossed on the sole that prevents them sliding backwards.

Nordic norm
The term denoting the standardized sizes and design of cross-country skis and boots.

Off-piste skiing
Skiing on slopes that are not marked or patrolled as opposed to skiing on prepared pistes.

Parallel open stepped swings
Turns initiated by stepping the inside ski parallel to the outside ski.

Parallel swings
Turns performed with the skis parallel at all times. The skis are unweighted and turned together, and there is no stemming out or stepping.

Pistes
Prepared ski runs classified as blue, red or black according to difficulty, with black being the most difficult. Pistes are signposted and patrolled.

Pole flip
A ballet manoeuvre where the skier, assisted by ski poles, performs a 360° rotation around a horizontal axis.

Pole plant
Planting the ski pole in the snow to aid skiing technique.

Poma lift see *Button lift*

Pop
The spring made by competitors in the aerial event at the point of takeoff to maximize potential air time so that flight is not just a consequence of inrun speed and jump profile.

Preparation phase
The part of the turn in which the skier prepares for the initiation phase. The movements may include, for example, opening the skis into a plough position.

Pressure
The force exerted through the skis to the snow by shifting weight from one ski to the other, or backwards and forwards. Also called weighting.

Ready position
The relaxed, poised position adopted in order to remain in dynamic balance, and to cope with turning forces and changes in terrain.

Rear-entry boot
An alternative to the traditional front-entry boot, the rear-entry variety which opens at the back is becoming increasingly popular.

Recco
A safety device which is attached to the back of a ski boot and reflects the signals transmitted by the Recco detector. It is used to detect skiers buried by an avalanche.

Reverse camber
The opposite of camber, reverse camber allows the ski to dig into the snow when performing carved turns.

Running groove
The narrow indentation along the length of the ski's base which aids the ski's stability on snow.

Running surface
The bottom surface or base of the ski.

Safety binding
The safety binding is a device used in Alpine skiing that enables the ski to come off automatically in a fall by releasing the boot.

Schussing
Also known as straight running, schussing involves skiing down the fall line.

Short swings
Short radius turns with parallel skis.

Side cut
The tapered mid-section, or waist, of the ski.

Sideslipping
A means of travelling sideways downhill by skidding the skis. It may be initiated in one of four ways: stepping downhill, downsinking, downsinking with leg rotation, and directing your knees downhill.

Sidestepping
A technique used for climbing uphill where the skis are stepped up the slope one at a time.

Ski évolutif
Taught in some areas of France, this is one of the short ski teaching methods whereby beginners are started on short skis and gradually progress to longer skis.

Ski poles
Used to aid balance and for support during skiing, ski poles are usually made of a light metal and come with a variety of hand grips and with or without straps.

Ski stopper
A device which prevents the ski sliding away when the boot is released from the binding.

Slalom
The shortest of the four World Cup disciplines, slalom is an event in which skiers must descend through the specially placed gates on the course as quickly as possible.

Snowboarding
A hybrid snow sport that combines surfing and skiing.

Snowplough
Also known as the wedge, the snowplough is formed by pushing the ski tips together and the tails apart. It is used mainly for regulating speed and changes of direction.

Snowplough turns
Turning in the snowplough position by transferring weight on to the outside ski. Weight on the right ski will change direction to the left, and vice versa.

Speed skiing
Also known as the 'Flying Kilometre' or 'KL' (Kilometre Lance), speed skiing is an event in which the competitors ski as fast as possible down a straight course using special equipment to aid speed and reduce wind resistance.

Spins
In freestyle, rotations around the vertical axis with the skis remaining on the snow.

Spread eagle
An upright freestyle jump where the legs and arms are held out to the side in a star position.

Star turn
A means of turning around on the flat where the skis are stepped around either the tails or the tips.

Steering phase
The third and final phase of the turn, which links up with the preparation phase of the next turn. Turns are steered mainly by applying pressure to the outside ski. However, angulation, banking and counter-rotation are also usually involved.

Step (skate) turns
A means of changing direction by stepping the skis out to the side. They are used extensively in cross-country skiing.

Stop swing
A quick and effective means of coming to a halt where the skis are suddenly turned uphill in a parallel position.

Super-G
The newest of the World Cup disciplines, the super-G is a cross between downhill and giant slalom.

Takeoff
In freestyle aerials, the movements of extension of the hips and knees with the simultaneous lifting of the arms for the purpose of maximizing the height of a jump trajectory. See also *Pop*.

Telemark turn
Invented by Sondre Norheim and named after the area of Norway in which he lived, the Telemark turn is a technique whereby the skier drops the inside knee. The inside ski trails behind and the outside (steering) ski leads.

Torsional stiffness
The term applied to the ski's ability to twist along its length.

Traversing
Skiing across the fall line.

Tuck position
A crouched position used when schussing, particularly in speed skiing and downhill racing, to minimize wind resistance.

Two-phase (diagonal) stride
The fundamental cross-country technique based on natural walking movements which are extended to enable forward gliding momentum over flat ground and up easy gradients.

Unweighting
Decreasing the friction between skis and snow by reducing the pressure (weight) on the skis. This makes it easier to turn the skis.

Uphill stem swings
Swings which are initiated in the traverse by stemming out the inside ski.

Upright
An aerial manoeuvre which does not involve any rotation around the horizontal axis. It may include rotation around the vertical axis (helicopter).

Waist
The tapered mid-section of the ski.

Wash-board
A series of equally-spaced, man-made bumps.

Wash-out
The sliding sideways of the skis throughout a turn.

Water jump
An aerial training facility made up of a synthetic inrun and kicker with a water landing. Wet or dry suits, helmets, skis and boots are worn.

White-out
A term referring to impaired visibility, usually due to low cloud, falling snow or fog.

Windblown snow
Snow that has been displaced by the wind and been made more compact, usually with a hard crust.

Index

Numerals in *italics* refer to illustrations

Index

Acknowledgements
We would like to thank the following for supplying photographs for use in the book:
Allsport: front cover and pages 53, 66, 81, 86, 93, 96, 99, 103, 108, 109, 116, 123, 124, 128, 129, 130, 132, 137
Robert Aschenbrenner: page 57
Atomic skis/Mark Shapiro: pages 7, 14, 20, 21, 85, 89, 101, 106, 111, 120, 136
Dunlop Footwear Ltd/Allsport: page 23
John Eddowes: pages 125, 127
Sarah Ferguson: pages 92, 131
Adrian Fox: front cover and pages 39, 102, 134
French Government Tourist Office: pages 27, 107, 110, 112
Doug Godlington: pages 118, 119
David Goldsmith: page 115
Grandstand Sports and Leisure: page 11
Italian State Tourist Office: pages 100, 104
Markitrade Ltd: page 122
Mast-Co Ltd: pages 9, 101
Nevica: pages 82, 101
Jeff O'Brien: pages 17, 56, 126

Raichle/Badger Sports: page 10
Recco/Badger Sports: page 22
Salomon Ski Equipment (GB) Ltd: pages 13, 32, 57, 80, 105, 113, 114
Mark Shapiro: back cover and pages 19, 94, 133
John Shedden: pages 25, 87, 91, 97
Snowbusiness Ltd: pages 9, 18, 84, 105
Swiss National Tourist Office (London): page 98
Swix/Badger Sports: pages 15, 90
Ron Whitby: pages 9, 57, 88

The special instructional photography featuring Jim Murray on the back cover and in Chapters 2, 3 and 4 was taken by Robert Aschenbrenner.

Bibliography
The centred skier, Denise McCluggage, Bantam Books (Chapters 2 and 6)
The handbook of skiing, Karl Gamma, Pelham Books (Chapters 2 and 3)
The inner game of tennis, Timothy W. Gallwey, Cape (Chapter 6)
Skiing: developing your skill, John Shedden, The Crowood Press (Chapter 6)
Skiing right, Horst Abraham, Johnson Books (Chapter 6)
Skilehrplan West Germany, Deutscher Verband für das Skilehrwesen, BLV Verlagsgesellschaft München (Chapters 2 and 3)
Skilful skiing, John Shedden, EP Publishing (Chapters 3 and 6)
Sporting body, sporting mind, Syer & Connelly, Cambridge University Press (Chapter 6)
Stretch and relax, Tobias & Stewart, Dorling Kindersley (Chapter 6)
Stretching, Bob Anderson, Pelham Books (Chapter 6)
World Cup ski technique, Major and Larsson, Poudre Publishing Company (Chapter 6)